Child Development in Practice

How should children feel about themselves and their learning? How do I know what children have learnt and how can I move them on? How can I ensure that resources are available for children to use actively and independently?

In today's busy setting an understanding of child development sometimes gets overlooked, yet it lies at the heart of effective practice. *Child Development in Practice* provides an approachable, user-friendly base from which to plan ways of working with children that are developmentally appropriate and will enable them to learn enjoyably and effectively.

Drawing on recent research, the book thoughtfully discusses sound principles of child development alongside descriptions of everyday practice. It then offers practical advice on how to fully utilise the key areas in an early years setting, including the creative area, books and stories and the outside, and shows how to plan and implement integrated topics where teaching is cross-curricular and holistic. Throughout, a series of key questions are presented to encourage practitioners to reflect on why they are teaching in certain ways and increase their understanding of children's developmental needs.

Directly linking theory and practice, this book aims to give students and practitioners the knowledge and confidence they need to help children become active, interactive and independent learners.

Pamela May is an Early Years Consultant.

Child Development in Practice

Responsive teaching and learning from birth to five

Pamela May

Routledge
Taylor & Francis Group

LONDON AND NEW YORK

This first edition published 2011
by Routledge
2 Park Square, Milton Park, Abingdon, Oxon, OX14 4RN

Simultaneously published in the USA and Canada
by Routledge
270 Madison Avenue, New York, NY 10016

Routledge is an imprint of the Taylor & Francis Group, an informa business

© 2011 Pamela May

Typeset in Optima by Glyph International
Printed and bound in Great Britain by
CPI Antony Rowe, Chippenhan, Wiltshire

British Library Cataloguing in Publication Data
A catalogue record for this book is available from the British Library

Library of Congress Cataloging-in-Publication Data
May, Pamela.
   Child development in practice : responsive teaching and learning from birth to five / by Pamela
   May. – 1st ed.
   p. cm.
   1. Early childhood education–United States. 2. Early childhood education–Curricula–United
   States. 3. Child development–United States. I. Title.
   LB1140.23.M37 2011
372.21–dc22   2010020464

ISBN13: 978-0-415-49753-4 (hbk)
ISBN13: 978-0-415-49755-8 (pbk)
ISBN13: 978-0-203-84062-7 (ebk)

Contents

Contents

Acknowledgements

I would like to thank Clair Stevens and the staff of Manor House Nursery School in Margate who provided the photographs of good practice that I have used to illustrate the text and who allowed me to visit their outstanding nursery, and Jacob Pagett for allowing me to include his letter to his Granddad John.

My thanks are also due to Toni Buchan for her permission to use photos of her son, Connor, and for giving so generously her time and expertise in advising on the structure and content of the book.

I would like to thank John May for his continued love and encouragement and for his editorial support. His current favourite book is *Scaredy Squirrel*.[1]

Every effort has been made to trace copyright holders of material reproduced in this book. Any right not acknowledged here will be acknowledged in subsequent printings if notice is given to the publishers.

I would like to dedicate this book to the memory of Dr Gill Bottle, a wonderful colleague and a dear friend.

Introduction

Children are whole people who have feelings, ideas, a sense of embodied self and relationships with others and who need to be physically, mentally, morally and spiritually healthy.[2]

The first place that I would take my specialist early years PGCE students was a local nursery school that would provide part of their school experience. The nursery head-teacher would ask the students to kneel down on the floor of the nursery. They were always disconcerted at this opening request, fearing some ritual for which they had not been adequately prepared. The headteacher then told the students to explore the setting on all fours and to note what they could see. It was when he explained that this was the view of the nursery that a young child saw that the rationale for his strange request became immediately apparent. This book is, in some ways, similar in that it looks at the early years nursery experience from the young child's point of view, from the inside of their heads, looking out, rather than from the outside, looking in, thus gaining an insight into how a child develops.

Why study child development?

Children's earliest years are vital to their subsequent success and well-being. Yet there are feelings of anxiety and confusion amongst parents and practitioners about how children should be treated and how childhoods should be lived. Historically, early years' educa-tion was linked to what was known about how children developed. As early as the Haddow Report in 1931 there was the exhortation that 'the curriculum of the primary school is to be thought of in terms of activity and experience rather than knowledge to be acquired and facts to be stored'.[3] Educators such as John Dewey were influential in placing child development at the heart of high-quality education for the youngest children in our education system. Attempts by recent governments to ensure children's educational progress has led, however, to a more target-based system of education, and this, together with the growth of competency-based training for practitioners, has had the effect of marginalising child development in both training and practice. Currently, national concerns about children's well-being and confidence are leading to a realisation that knowledge about children's emotional, social, physical and cognitive development may well lead, not only to happier children but also to children who learn more successfully. At this point, it needs to be emphasised that there is a difference between children's *development* and their *progress*. Children's development is the study of how they change emotionally, cognitively, physically and socially as they grow; and the study of how these changes are affected by both environmental and genetic factors. This is very different from the progress that they make through the Stepping Stones of the Early Years Foundation Stage (EYFS). The Stepping Stones sometimes follow children's natural development but very often do not. They are predominantly about the acquisition of academic bodies of knowledge such as reading, computation and the humanities.

This book maintains that, both to develop to their full developmental potential and to progress effectively through the EYFS, children need first, to feel good about themselves as people and second, to develop those attributes that all effective learners have: namely, motivation, self-confidence and social competency. Thus, the major aim of this book is to suggest ways in which practitioners can, through their relationships with their children, help them become these effective learners.

Currently, children's educational progress has a high profile and, as a result, many research studies are being conducted to establish the type of environment in which they are most likely to flourish. These studies are often reported in the press as having clear indications as to what benefits one type of care may have over another. Some studies will suggest, for example, that day care is inappropriate for the very youngest children,[4] while another study suggests that grandparents are not as able to prepare their grandchildren for school as effectively as nurseries.[5] This book suggests that where a child is placed in their early years is of secondary importance to what happens to them while they are there. In other words, children may be well cared for and educated across a range of settings and situations, be they domestic, state, private or voluntary. What makes a significant difference to their learning success is the quality of practitioner training. This needs to include a secure understanding of child development, as it has been defined, above, as this is the key to ensuring that children's needs are met wherever they find themselves. Meeting these developmental needs is of vital importance in helping them flourish as successful learners.

Child development is not, then, about teaching the bodies of knowledge that need to be addressed in the Foundation Stage. Rather, it is about **how** that knowledge should be taught to very young children in ways that link to their natural innate development.[6] This was a major finding of the Rumbold Report, which reported in 1990, and which investigated the quality of experiences offered to young children in early years settings. Developmentally appropriate practice, as it is sometimes called, comes from respected research and theory and is enshrined in current government legislation. From this research and theory we can extract clear principles of practice which guide our practice. We should ask ourselves 'If I believe in this theory, how would my setting look to reflect it?'. In this way, we can link theory directly to practice and enable children to learn successfully.

In fact the reasons why our settings look as they do – why they have role-play areas, sand and water play, and an outside area for example – are not random. Each aspect of the early years setting is based on a theory. In other words, researchers have suggested, through their observations of children's behaviour, that certain experiences help children to learn most effectively and the way we, as practitioners, offer these experiences to children depends on our knowledge and our beliefs about children's development and ways of learning. These theories are the 'big ideas' on which our everyday practice is based and the first four chapters will explore them and consider how they underpin what we do every day.

What we know and believe about how children learn best is evident in how our setting looks. If we think that children learn best by sitting down and practising their writing skills in a formal way, there will be tables and chairs for each child. If we believe that children learn best by being active, then we will have less furniture but a range of interesting things to do that involve first-hand, practical involvement from the children. This latter approach reflects much of the research by Jean Piaget and Lev Vygotsky early in the twentieth century. It became apparent to them that the mind of the young child gathers not only basic numerical, scientific and linguistic information but also strategies for remembering, understanding and solving problems if they are learning actively. If this is what we believe, then there must be activities and experiences in our settings that will engage children's interest for prolonged periods of time to allow for creative thinking and a deep level of learning. This will have direct implications for how we organise our setting and how we manage children's learning. Theories are only helpful to further young children's learning if they have implications for our everyday practice!

This book acknowledges the principles of child development which were devised by the National Association for the Education of Young Children (NYEYC),[7] and are stated below:

1. All the domains of development and learning – physical, social and emotional, and cognitive – are important, and they are closely interrelated. Children's development and learning in one domain influence and are influenced by what takes place in other domains.
2. Many aspects of children's learning and development follow well-documented sequences, with later abilities, skills and knowledge building on those already acquired.
3. Development and learning proceed at varying rates from child to child, as well as at uneven rates across different areas of a child's individual functioning.
4. Development and learning result from a dynamic and continuous interaction of biological maturation and experience.
5. Early experiences have profound effects, both cumulative and delayed, on a child's development and learning; and optimal periods exist for certain types of development and learning to occur.
6. Development proceeds towards greater complexity, self-regulation, and symbolic or representational capacities.
7. Children develop best when they have secure, consistent relationships with responsive adults and opportunities for positive relationships with peers.
8. Development and learning occur in and are influenced by multiple social and cultural contexts.

9. Always mentally active in seeking to understand the world around them, children learn in a variety of ways; a wide range of teaching strategies and interactions are effective in supporting all these kinds of learning.
10. Play is an important vehicle for developing self-regulation as well as for promoting language, cognition and social competence.
11. Development and learning advance when children are challenged to achieve at a level just beyond their current mastery, and also when they have many opportunities to practice newly acquired skills.
12. Children's experiences shape their motivation and approaches to learning, such as persistence, initiative and flexibility; in turn, these dispositions and behaviours affect their learning and development.

In this book, Chapters 1–4 consider the theories of child development and discuss the knowledge that early years specialists need to understand in order to teach young children effectively. While recognising that children's development is multifaceted, there are four strands which will be looked at in depth. These are children's:

- emotional and behavioural development
- cognitive and intellectual development
- physical and motor development
- social and language development.

From these strands, practitioner questions have been extracted which, it is hoped, may be helpful when they are planning and evaluating their provision. These are:

- How should children feel about themselves and their learning? *This links to children's emotional and behavioural development.*
- How do I know where the children are in their learning and how can I move them on? *This links to children's cognitive and intellectual development.*
- How can I ensure that resources are available for children to use actively and independently? *This links to children's physical and motor development.*
- How should we all act towards each other? *This links to children's social and language development.*

These questions are designed to encourage a reflective attitude to practice and, although designed to highlight *children's* development, will also have some implications for how practitioners feel about themselves, their colleagues and their practice. How children feel and act towards each other in the setting will directly reflect how the adults feel and act towards each other!

The next six chapters of the book take these strands and their associated questions and apply them directly to areas of practice that are common in all settings. In these chapters there will be direct links to the Practice Guidance and Statutory Requirements of the Early Years Foundation Stage. As this is referred to constantly throughout the book, it is impossible to index practically. In all the chapters the six areas of learning and development are referred to by their abbreviations:

PSE	Personal, Social and emotional development
CLL	Communication, language and literacy
PSRN	Problem solving, reasoning and numeracy
KUW	Knowledge and understanding of the world
PD	Physical development
CD	Creative development.

The strands and questions have been separated out purely to help practitioners consider them in some depth. In reality, of course, they intertwine and children all progress at different rates and often in different directions from that anticipated by the practitioner. In the last chapter, the strands will be gathered into themes which practitioners may like to consider when planning holistic learning. These themes will provide opportunities for children to follow their own interests at a level which is appropriate for them as individuals through the playful ways in which they are presented.

The EYFS consistently reminds us that child development is at the heart of effective practice. It also states that child development is complex and individual to each child: 'Development is a continuous, complex interaction of environmental and genetic factors in which the body, brain and behaviour become more complex'.[8] This book, then, aims to explore these interactions and to suggest practical ways in which children can be enabled to become more successful as learners and more confident as human beings.

Section 1 The theory of child development

1 Children's emotional and behavioural development

Ideas about children's well-being, motivation and creativity are currently high on the national agenda with a range of debates such as 'Lost Childhoods' which began in the *Daily Telegraph* on 12 September 2006 and the discussion on 'happiness' by Nel Noddings, where she talks of happiness as being 'an aim of life and education'.[9]

Government has mirrored the national debate by legislation and initiatives such as 'All Our Futures, Creative and Cultural Education'[10] and 'Every Child Matters'.[11] 'All Our Futures', states that 'When individuals find their creative strengths, it can have an enormous impact on overall achievement'[12] making clear the links between motivation, creativity and high achievement. This report also supports the idea that we need to build on children's talents and interests by saying that 'the key is to find what children are good at. Self-confidence and self-esteem then tend to rise and overall performance improves'.[13] Clearly, government is recognising that if children feel good about themselves and what they are doing, their learning will be more successful.

In this chapter we will consider what theory and current research tell us about children's emotions and how their views about themselves as people directly affect their success as learners. In major reports on early years education in England – from '*Starting with Quality*' (*The Rumbold Report*) published in 1990, the Startright Report, published in 1994, through to the recently published Cambridge Review, published in 2009 – researchers have commented on the impact of children's well-being, empowerment and self-esteem on their motivation to learn. Sir Christopher Ball states categorically that 'The art of learning is not a mystery. No-one learns effectively without motivation, social skills and confidence – and very few fail to learn successfully if they have developed these enabling attitudes and 'super skills' of learning.[14] No mention here, then, of needing a high IQ to be good at learning; but one must have self-confidence and be able to get along with others. Similarly, Robin Alexander in his address as part of the Cambridge Primary Review, 'Emerging Perspectives on Childhood'[15] explores the notion that adopting a policy of empowerment for children would help to rid us of a view of children that is negative and deficit: i.e. they are seen as passive, problematic and weak. The current EYFS document happily supports the alternative view: that children should be seen as competent and eager to engage with the world. This view presents the child as strong and with huge potential, always providing that there are trusted companions who will learn alongside the child and that the child is in a stimulating and rich environment.

EYFS cards 2.1, 2.3 and 2.4 explicitly support this positive view of the young child. The current theories that underpin this positive and uplifting view of childhood come mainly from the English 'Birth to Three Matters Framework', Scandinavian countries and from New Zealand and Reggio Emilia in Northern Italy.

Self-esteem

Self-esteem is the picture you have of yourself, your abilities, your social competence and your looks. Children who feel that they can accomplish what they set out to do, who know that there are people who want to be with them are said to have high self-esteem. This self-picture has been put together since birth and is formed by how people who are important to the children, have responded to them.

Self-esteem will not remain static and young children, who, with their lack of experience, will need continuous encouragement to build up the confidence that will promote a good self-image. Children will feel differently about themselves in different situations: for example, in their family, in their early years setting or with their friends. Of course, these experiences are part and parcel of normal life and are counter-balanced by a secure family environment with the constancy it provides of love, acceptance and boundaries of behaviour. This consistency gives children an indicator of their value and worth and leads to a strong sense of identity. Children will come to our settings with a fairly clear sense of their identity and their strengths and weaknesses, even though, of course, they will not be able to articulate these. A practitioner will learn about a child's self-belief through the ways in which the child behaves. One of the key ways that a child is helped to feel confident is to feel secure in his surroundings. Children, who have a stable family life have already been provided with a positive, continuing sense of their identity. The job of the practitioner is to provide ongoing continuity and stability so that all children feel that they belong to the setting too and that they are in a place where their self-image is reinforced and enhanced. Consequently, their self-confidence can grow. This requirement becomes much more challenging, of course, when there are children in the setting whose early experiences have been fractured or unstable, so that they come to the setting with no clear idea as to who they are, what they are good at or what might be expected of them. These are children who have low self-esteem, feel insecure and who probably have a low view of their abilities and will therefore not risk any activity in which they are likely to fail.

As emotional well-being is now recognised to be central to children's success as learners, it is essential that planning for every area in the setting takes into account children's emotional needs and each succeeding chapter in the book will reflect this by asking the related practitioner's question, 'How should children feel about themselves and their learning?'

The requirement of the EYFS to allocate a key person to each child also reflects the crucial importance that is attached to helping children feel secure, safe and confident in their surroundings. Marion Dowling, in her book entitled *Young Children's Personal,*

Social and Emotional Development states that 'One of the most important gifts we can offer young children is a positive view of themselves. Without this they will flounder through life and be constantly seeking reassurance from others as they cannot seek it from within'.[16]

Well-being

The EYFS supports the notion of security and love by requiring that each child in the EYFS is linked to a loving and dependable adult by stating that 'Babies and children become independent by being able to rely upon adults for reassurance and comfort'.[17] It is within these close, loving relationships that reassurance and comfort are fostered and it is these feelings that give children the security, safety and confidence that they need to begin their journey towards well-being and independence. A secure attachment to a caregiver (or a key person) provides children with a sense of well-being which is thought to provide a buffer to the effects of stress. Children with a poor or disorganised attachment show raised levels of the cortisol hormone that tend to limit their ability to function effectively both emotionally and cognitively. It is worth, at this point, making the distinction between a key worker and a key person. Elfer *et al.*[18] argue that 'key worker' and a 'key person' are not interchangeable terms although they are often used as such. A key worker describes a liaising role which concentrates on enabling a range of professionals to work in a coordinated way. The key person, on the other hand, is primarily an emotional relationship whose focus is the well-being and security of the child.

Well-being, then, is not about things in life going well; most of us are able to cope reasonably well when life is progressing smoothly. Children with high levels of well-being are able to 'stay on top of things' when the going gets tough and things are going badly. They show more resilience to the effects of events that most people experience at various points in their lives, such as ill-health, the loss of a loved one or other significant changes. Resilience has been defined as 'normal development under difficult circumstances'.[19]

Agency

Well-being is usually felt when children have some 'agency' or freedom of choice about what they are doing in the setting. This idea of autonomy and freedom of choice resonates with the characteristics upon which a democratic society largely depends, characteristics such as independence, cooperation and freedom of thought.

Bronwyn Davies (1990), refers to agency as 'a sense of oneself as one who can go beyond the given meanings in any one discourse and forge something new'.[20] Children with a lack of agency tend to believe that their talents and abilities are set in stone and invariable, whereas those with a sense of agency believe that their talents and abilities can develop over time and will respond positively to new and interesting experiences they encounter and to the effort that they expend.

Belonging and boundaries

[handwritten: asked to send xmas cards]

These can also be thought of as part of well-being. Children who feel that they belong to their setting have a good sense of well-being. Children can often be heard saying 'At my nursery…', and this phrase is an indicator that they feel they belong to the setting and are at home there. This feeling is essentially associated to the loving relationship that the key person offers and is evidence of the secure relationships and friendships that the child has formed there. Boundaries are the expectations, rules and responsibilities that come with belonging to a group, be it family, nursery, faith or cultural. Every organisation has its expectations and knowing what these are help a child to feel 'contained' and safe. The most important aspect of expectations, rules and responsibilities is that they are consistent, so that the young child can begin to understand what is acceptable behaviour and follow the code that is in place. It is when children feel secure and have a good level of well-being that their behaviour is most likely to be positive. Behaviour, then, is always linked directly to how the child is feeling. Challenging behaviour is never random but stems from an emotional cause which staff need to try to understand before efforts are made to manage it. Managing a child's difficult behaviour without having some understanding of a possible cause may well lead to a situation where an undesirable action is temporarily controlled but the child's emotional need has not been addressed. As Rosie Roberts states in *Self-Esteem and Early learning*; 'unreasonable behaviour is almost always reasonable from the point of view of the person doing it'.[21] This phrase is really helpful as it suggests that practitioners consider and attempt to understand the situation from the child's point of view as a starting point to the management of it.

Communication

Children who are secure because they feel that they belong to their setting are likely to talk freely and confidently to adults and to their friends about what interests them. The aspect of agency that is a part of well-being gives children the confidence to explore new ideas and to share them with all who show an interest! It is these twin strands of security and confidence that give children the motivation to communicate experiences that are meaningful. They will do this in a range of ways such as role play, small-world play, painting, singing and mark-making. Tina Bruce calls this process 'representation'[22] as children re-present their important ideas and experiences. Children are unlikely to feel able to do this unless they are emotionally secure.

[handwritten: Jumping from. Side wall unaided]

Positive dispositions

A high self-esteem will give children the confidence that they will need to succeed in learning something new. Learning a new skill or attempting to understand some new knowledge requires all of us to take a 'leap of faith'. The leap is from something that is known and familiar, and therefore comfortable, to something that is unknown and possibly challenging and scary. To embark on this journey sometimes requires nerves of steel; just think about the adult learning to drive or trying to master a new language! The inner voice that tells us 'Yes, *I can do this*' is called a positive disposition and is the driving force that helps us to get started and to persevere when the going gets tough. Lilian Katz calls a positive disposition a *'pattern of behaviour'* or a habit of mind.[23] She suggests that children may have inherent aptitudes and talents but may not necessarily use them. The disposition is the motivation to apply their talent so that they habitually feel positive about their abilities. For a child to feel positive about learning something new there needs to be both a cognitive challenge – i.e. something that awakens the child's curiosity – and the desire to learn. An example of this might be as complex as learning to read or as simple as balancing on a log in the setting's outside area. Each of these skills has two major strands that need mastering: the 'thinking' strand, where the child assesses that this is something that she can realistically attempt, and the 'feeling' strand, where she experiences the strong desire to try. Jennie Lindon calls positive dispositions 'where thinking meets feeling'[24] and it is a beautiful description of learning that happens every day in early years settings.

Currently in schools there is a danger that the balance between thinking and feeling has not been maintained and that too much emphasis has been placed on 'thinking' and not enough on the 'feeling' part of the process. Lilian Katz goes on to explain, for example, that children who can successfully decode print (the thinking aspect) may not necessarily go on to become self-motivated readers if the joy of the story (the feeling part) is buried beneath a search for capital letters and full stops.

In this section we have concentrated on considering the 'feeling' part of learning as it links to children's self-esteem. In the cognitive chapter to follow there will be a discussion about the 'thinking' aspect of dispositions as it links to children's understanding.

Struggling children

If we have children in our setting who appear emotionally vulnerable and do not appear to be thriving, it may be worth considering that this might be for one of the following reasons:

- There may be inappropriate challenges at which they know they may fail (e.g. a requirement to record learning by writing or drawing on paper). This is particularly likely if there is an emphasis on formal learning.
- There may be inconsistencies in the setting that send confusing messages about self-image and expectations, (e.g. a work/play divide or differences in attitudes within the team of practitioners).
- There may be inappropriate separations from people who are important to the child and upon whom they rely for security.
- There may be a lack of richness and stimulation which closes down curiosity and leads to passivity.

Children who appear not to have a positive disposition to learning are often referred to as 'disaffected'. Julie Fisher (*Starting from the Child*) suggests that in fact, very young children are naturally 'affected' or eager to learn.[25] It is some aspects of their school experience that causes them to lose their affection. The following aspects are some of the things that children find most difficult to cope with:

- not being listened to
- not enough time
- a disorganised environment
- no clear or consistent rules
- not having their work valued
- disconnected or 'disembedded' learning. (i.e. learning that is not meaningful to the child).

How does play help children's emotional development?

If children are to be successful learners, the process of learning has to be broadly enjoyable. One of the delights of having a hobby as an adult is that we are engaged in

'Enjoyment is a powerful motivator'

something we enjoy doing. We often lose track of time while we are busy with our hobby and are sorry when we have to stop.

This is just how children feel about play and this enjoyment is a powerful motivator. The adult's hobby is usually pitched at a level that is challenging but achievable and the adult usually has some choice over the level of activity chosen (think of starting at the beginner's French class, and progressing to the intermediate and then the advanced one). Play is also this flexible and allows a child to join at a level that is just right for them and then to take it to a higher level. With play, children can act at a much higher level than they are able to in real life, allowing them to drive trains, bath the baby or be a shop-keeper. This facility to be in control and operate at a 'grown-up' level gives a child's self-esteem and confidence a significant boost and is hugely satisfying emotionally. One of the strengths of play as a process is that it cannot be directed by an adult and is in the genuine control of the young child. Thus, a child is empowered to make decisions, plan the game, choose the participants, select the equipment needed and gain compe-tence at those things which interest her. A successful learner needs to develop attitudes that result in high motivation, an ability to persist, an ability to solve problems and think imaginatively. All of these things are most happily to be found in children's play!

Children's cognitive and intellectual development

2

A possible definition of cognition is 'The mental process of knowing, including aspects such as awareness, perception, reasoning and judgement. It is the process by which a person learns and it involves strategies for problem-solving and creative and critical thinking'.[26]

Cognition is the 'thinking' part of a disposition. A disposition is considered to consist of two aspects – one is thinking and the other is feeling. Margaret Carr suggests that children who have a positive disposition to learning are 'ready, willing and able to learn'.[27] One of the major aspects of children's *ability* to learn is their curiosity and it is this which acts as a driving force in their search for meaning.

Coupled with curiosity is the sense of agency that we encountered when we were considering children's emotional development in Chapter 1. If children feel that they can progress in their understanding and that they have some control of their learning process, they are much more likely to attempt something new or persist at something which is a challenge than if they don't feel confident and are being asked to learn passively. Curiosity and agency, then, are two key drivers to cognitive development.

Learning new knowledge

Young children always find that new knowledge makes more sense if it is linked to something within their own experience. New knowledge, for them, needs to have a purpose; this has sometimes been called 'knowing how' rather than 'knowing that'.[28] This is the kind of knowledge that might help a child to construct a model or plant a bulb. The child needs to know the different qualities between Sellotape and glue or which way up a bulb should be planted for it to grow. Here, new knowledge is attached to an immediate problem which needs to be solved (knowing 'how'), so the knowledge is purposeful. New knowledge which is separated from a purpose (sometimes called academic knowledge or knowing 'that' such as, perhaps, a written sum in symbolic form $3 + 2 = ?$) is not embedded in any meaning for the child who lacks both the curiosity and the agency to persist. Learning of this sort does not enable the child to make connections with what they already know and can easily lead to the disaffection mentioned above.[29] Margaret Donaldson discusses just this point and argues that children can understand complex ideas if they are presented, or 'embedded' in experiences that children can relate to.[30] For very young children these are nearly always practical, first-hand and active experiences connected to the ways in which they lead their daily lives. We shall consider, in each of the following chapters, how this theory works in practice in the different areas of the early years setting and how children can come to understand a range of concepts in ways that make sense to them.

Bruner's spiral curriculum

Jerome Bruner suggested a model for learning that can be thought of as a spiral, rather like one of those old-fashioned bed springs! Children approach new learning at the lower end of the spiral, taking to the learning experience what they already know and have experienced. If the learning experiences stay constant – i.e. that they are regularly available – children can revisit them taking their increased maturity and knowledge and learn at a more sophisticated level. To continue with the picture of the spiral, the child might by now be half-way to the top. Thus, the child who has constant access to powder paint can advance from discovering how much water needs to be added to make the right consistency to mixing paints just the right colour to match the tone needed for a painting. Bruner believed that any knowledge could be taught to any child as long as it was honestly and appropriately done. In the early years setting, then, children can begin to use alternating patterns by printing with an apple and then a pear and continue the pattern. They will not know that this alternating binary pattern is the beginning of algebra, but they are absorbing a concept that will be of great use to them later on in their lives.

Social constructivism

As curiosity and agency are key aspects of learning new knowledge, they suggest a theory of learning which is primarily active. It was Jean Piaget who first observed young learners scientifically and noted that they made sense of their world by being what he called 'lone scientists'. Each child, he discovered, made or constructed, knowledge individually, depending upon their own experiences, interests and abilities. Just as every adult takes something different from a novel or a film, depending on their individual tastes, needs and interests, so each child constructs their own understanding from their experiences.

This view of learning reflects the oft quoted Chinese proverb: 'I hear and I forget, I see and I remember, I do and I understand'.[31] From this theory we can deduce that although we can expect some particular learning to come from an experience we organise in our settings, the reality is that children are unique[32] and each child will take something different from that experience according to their level of development. It is for this reason that the most successful learning experiences we create are open-ended and flexible, providing children with a wide range of learning opportunities and plenty of time to explore the experience fully. What we often expect, however, is right

17

or wrong answers and a short time frame in which to work. These kinds of more flexible experiences are often referred to as 'ongoing provision', as opposed to 'activities', and they include role play, small-world play, outdoor play, painting and drawing, model making, music making and block play; anything, in fact, where it is the children who are in control and can thus take the play where they need to for their own satisfaction.

Creativity and thinking skills

The type of open-ended provision described above provides children with just the kind of experiences they need to develop their creative skills and to learn how to think more deeply and laterally about what they are engaged in. If, for example, a large amount of wet sand and water can be used together in a setting, children have opportunities to learn, among other things, about consistency of materials, the qualities of wet sand, the nature of water flowing through sand and ways of blocking water flow. The learning will probably be encased in dramatic role play as Playmobile cars and people are swept along with the flow of water, only to be blocked by dams along the way! This type of deeply engaging play, sometimes known as 'free flow play', and requiring children to bring to it all that they know, feel and can do, is a high level of learning. Maria Robinson suggests that 'creativity is a process of seeing new possibilities',[33] the suggestion being that something new is forged from something that already exists. Making connections between already-learned knowledge and something new is at the heart of cognitive development and will most readily occur when areas in the setting are richly resourced. It is important to note that creativity in young children is almost never about an end product but is concerned with the process of production. It is at its most successful when a relationship is forged between knowing and feeling: i.e. the disposition that we considered earlier. The necessity to finalise every creation with something finished – as proof of the effort that has gone into creating is, in itself, counterproductive and may very well lead children to avoid committing to a creative process if they are routinely asked either what the creation is intended to be or pressed for 'something to show mummy'.

Similarly, creativity is not about pleasing adults but about a creative act that is completely original. As the EYFS reminds us, 'It is difficult to make creative connections in learning when colouring in a worksheet or making a Diwali card just like everyone else'.[34]

To become creative, a child needs to develop a mindset of originality. The attributes that we have discussed in the section on children's emotional development give some suggestions as to how children need to feel about themselves and their abilities before they have the confidence to think 'outside the box'. The following attitudes to learning are some of the ones that will help a child to consider trying something new or tackling something from a different angle:

- concentration (spending a long time playing at one activity)
- problem-solving (thinking of different ways to try things)

- patience (being calm and persistent)
- self-confidence (expecting success but accepting failure as part of the learning process)
- enthusiasm (being cheerful and enjoying a challenge).[35]

Brains and minds

The brain

Technological advances in neuroscience have enabled researchers to understand the workings of the infant brain to a much greater degree. It is now accepted that babies' brains are genetically wired at birth but, although most of the neurons are present at this point, the richness of the connections between neurons that are made by the growing infant depend to a large extent on the experiences that the infant encounters. In fact, so influential are children's experiences on their development, it is now thought that experiences alter the very fabric or architecture of the brain and can be directly related to an increase or decrease in IQ measurements.[36] The brain's purpose is to receive and assimilate information quickly. However, in early years settings, fast-paced, logical learning should be used sparingly, perhaps at group times to teach children how to use tools safely or to teach a new song or rhyme. It is not a form of learning that young children can cope with for more than few minutes at a time as they are by nature active learners and this type of instructional teaching normally requires them to be still and passive. Children will soon become restless and disaffected and the wise practitioners will recognise children's inattention as a sign that too much instruction is developmentally inappropriate.

The art of providing a learning setting that is stimulating enough to engage children but not too intensive is not easily achieved. It is acquired by regularly observing how responsive children are to what is provided and being taking care to build in 'down time' for consolidation and practice as a balance to providing exciting and new challenges. What neuroscience has taught us is that young children cannot be made 'smarter' by intensive teaching or by the popular CDs that are on the market, which are designed to increase intelligence. Babies and young children are best helped to progress in their learning by being in a safe, yet interesting, environment in the company of people who will genuinely share their interests and enjoy learning alongside them.

The mind

The *mind* is different from the *brain*. In that it fulfils a separate function to the brain and is concerned with a 'looser' type of learning: i.e. the mind processes information that has been received by the brain. It interprets and reflects on the implications of new knowledge. It is the mind that considers reasons and makes judgements based on information that the brain has received. The processes that take place in the mind are slow, considered and complex and require children to spend considerable lengths of time, usually unconsciously, making sense of the new knowledge they have received and going through a process of what Jean Piaget called 'adaption, assimilation and accommodation'. It is not a quick process to receive new information, work out how it fits in with what is known already and decide whether what the child understands will change as a result of this new information. Often when we see children inactive in our settings, they may well be contemplating, reflecting and trying to make sense of some new piece of knowledge.

Cognitive milestones

Children develop at different rates, but all go through certain stages that it is helpful for practitioners to recognise. Some of the stages are outlined below.

Object permanence

For those working with babies, one of the earliest cognitive stages that is seen is known as *object permanence,* which is linked to the growing memory. Babies of 10–11 months, or thereabouts, begin to fret when their parent or carer leaves, as this developing concept of 'here or not here' leads to separation anxiety. Babies who are well attached to their parent or carer often show anger and reject the parent when they return. Practitioners need to know that this is a normal reaction and that it is babies who are indifferent to their returning carer who may be emotionally more vulnerable. Games such as 'peep-bo' and hiding objects help babies to practice this concept so that they begin to realise that comings and goings are normal and that the person who goes will come back again.

Separate identity

This concept tends to develop at around 18 months. The young child will sometimes need a transition object to fill the gap between 'me' and 'not me' and find a comforter an essential travelling companion. A child at this stage will begin to identify parts of their body and their language begins to reflect their separateness in the use of phrases such as 'Susie book', 'I cold', etc. It is at this point that picture books showing dressing and undressing such as How do I Put it On?,[37] and stories of everyday trips, such as Going to the Park,[38] strike a chord with young children whose experiences are largely defined by routine events such as these.

Symbolic thought

This is one of the most profound developments in young children's cognitive development. From the moment that a young child can hold a brick to his or her ear and say, 'Hello?', they demonstrate that they can use a simple object and activity to represent more complex ones. This single concept provides the foundation for the ability to imagine and to be creative. The child will begin perhaps to 'feed the baby' by pushing a spoon towards a doll's face or recognise that a picture of a ball in a book represents the object they have played with. It is this recognition and understanding of symbolism that will unlock for the developing child the worlds of literacy, mathematics, the creative arts and science. Usually the understanding of the concept of symbolism develops alongside spoken language, as the child searches to find words to accompany their play experiences. In role play in particular, the child will hold long conversations 'in role' about bathing the baby or driving the train – all experiences that, although far above their ability to undertake in real life, become hugely enjoyable and, more importantly perhaps, achievable, in the world of make believe.

Symbolic thought is not a concept to be rushed! Before children can reason symbolically, which requires them to be able to carry complex ideas in their heads, they need external and visible reminders of the ideas they are wrestling with. Consider an adult who needs to find an unfamiliar destination. A map provides an external and visible prop which helps them arrive at the correct address. Only after several trips to the same place are they confident enough to leave the map at home as they are sure that they have remembered the way. Children are just like this with many concepts, needing these props (or concept maps). These could be such things as counters when learning to count, picture clues when learning to read or lots of practice playing with pouring water before the concept of the direction of water flow is established without doubt. We should be wary of expecting young children to learn effectively without these props, as concepts that are not securely embedded at this stage provide poor foundations for subsequent learning. In each area of the early years setting, therefore, we will see learning opportunities which are practical, progressive and available for long periods of time so that children can revisit and practice what they are coming to know.

Schemas

Anne Meade and Pam Cubey (1995) defined schemas as 'cognitive structures or forms of thought – behaviour or in their drawings and paintings, indicate threads (schemas) running through them'.[39] Cathy Nutbrown, in her book entitled 'Threads of Thinking' explores the same phenomena and explores, through her professional observations of children, what she describes as 'the riches of children's minds'.[40] Certainly, children's learning of new concepts and knowledge is greatly enhanced if practitioners recognise and support children's schematic play by resourcing it and encouraging its development. Often a child will become dedicated to exploring one particular concept through a schema: for example, an 'enclosure' schema. A watchful practitioner will see evidence of an enclosure schema in a range of a child's behaviour and creative activities as they fill boxes with small objects such as beads, and then spend as much time as possible in a 'cave' or tent and perhaps make patterns with edges and borders. A child exploring the concept of circles may spend much time in the home corner, 'stirring the soup round and round', painting circular shapes and dancing in circles.

Schemas provide visual or external reminders of an internal concept or idea being learned and, just as we, as adults, make a shopping list to help us when we cannot carry a lot of information in our heads, young children wrestling with new ideas need these external props to help them until the concept is fully grasped and embedded in their minds. Schematic play naturally comes to an end when the new knowledge is securely understood. Piaget called the process of gaining new knowledge 'assimilation and accommodation'.

Assimilation is the process by which a person takes material into their mind from the environment; a struggle often follows as the new knowledge is fitted into what is already known. This is sometimes called 'cognitive dissonance' and is a healthy process by which new knowledge is assessed. If the new knowledge is accepted, the difference made to one's mind is known as accommodation, as the mind adjusts to the new understanding.

One of the endearing aspects of working with young children is the large number of 'misconstructs' that they make in the process of trying to make sense of their world. The 3 and 4 year old's life is full of partly understood ideas, not through lack of intelligence but because of lack of experience. An example that I particularly like is the reply a 4-year-old girl gave to her mother when asked what she and grandpa had been doing during a morning spent ploughing a field on grandpa's farm with a flock of white birds following the tractor. The reply came after a thoughtful pause: 'We were digging up seagulls'.

The mind can be thought of as a jigsaw. All of us have one but each one of us has a different number of pieces securely attached! Each child is constructing their own individual jigsaw according to their experiences, abilities and interests and schemas are a powerful aid to filling in more pieces of the jigsaw. We will consider how to resource the areas of our settings to enable children to explore their schemas in the ensuing chapters.

Theory of mind

This cognitive milestone, first researched by Alan Leslie in 1985, affects children in two important ways. It can be defined as the realisation that other people may see the world from a different perspective, have a different point of view and feel differently about the things that happen to them. Children are usually thought to be egocentric until the age of about 4 so that when, for example, a young child is asked where the sun goes at night, the reply will often be 'to bed' because that is what happens to them. Practitioners will sometimes find themselves trying to intervene in a quarrel where a 3 years old has removed the brick she needs from a friend's castle because it is just the one she needs for hers. These children may be developmentally unable to understand the anger and distress caused by their actions as they cannot see the situation from the other's point of view. Pleas to 'share nicely' may well fall on deaf ears at this stage in a child's development! Much better to gently try to explain the feelings of the other child so that the perpetrator can be helped towards gaining a theory of mind and an awareness of other people's feelings. This is the point in children's lives when they will proudly give a key person a creative offering with no understanding that the recipient may have little insight into its value. Many an adult has retrieved a scribble from the bin as an outraged 3 years old has protested that this is a valuable gift! We will, in Chapter 7, consider appropriate conversations that we can have with children about their creations which will preserve their pride and extend their thinking about the process of constructing their creations.

The second way in which theory of mind can affect children is that they start to develop deep friendships. At this point, practitioners will see these children playing cooperatively for the first time and not just playing individually alongside each other. Children will often seek out a special friend to play with and be genuinely deeply upset when they are separated. Adult staff will need to monitor these friendships as they provide rich opportunities for children to learn from and with a new friend, sometimes these new friendships are unbalanced in their intensity, with one child needing to dominate or be supported by the other.

Learning a concept

The business of learning a new concept is complex and can be thought of as a progression through several stages. To begin to understand what, for example, a ball is, the young child needs to experience it. Often a very young child will discover with some delight that throwing it out of the pushchair results in a patient adult returning it time and time again! This adult then attaches the spoken language to the object and thus the child learns that the object has a name and that it is called a 'ball'. Pictures of balls in books soon become recognisable as a symbolic representation of the object, but it is only very much later that the written word can be recognised as a different style of symbolic representation. The decoding of print, or 'reading', is a complex skill and often problematic for the young child, particularly if the preceding stages have been hurried through and the child has an insecure grasp of the object itself and its attached name from lack of experience. This is why the early years setting needs to concentrate all its efforts on giving children first-hand experiences of real objects and then helping them to name them and talk about them before expecting them to be able to read and write about them.

Concepts are not static: they grow and change as a person gains more experience and maturity of thought. The concept of a 'ball' is a rather simple one, as its properties remain constant, i.e. it is always round and it always rolls. In the teacher's guide to kindergarten, the concept of *parent* is described as 'being coloured by your experience with your own parent and other parents you know. Your concepts will certainly change and grow if you become a parent yourself and will continue to grow as your children grow up, especially if you have a child who, in her/his turn becomes a parent'.[41] A concept, then, is not the same thing as a fact; it is, rather, a secure understanding, a belief that is tested out many times to ensure its reliability. It is an individual's interpretation about an idea and, depending upon the nature of the concept, it may remain the same, as with

'Giving children first-hand experiences of real objects'

gravity or capacity; or may shift, such as with the concepts of mother or beauty. These are more subjective ideas and coloured by experience.

How does play help a child's cognitive development?

Play is the most effective way in which children learn new concepts. Through playful activities they are able to make their own connections between that which they already know and new concepts that they are encountering. We have considered how schematic play gives children opportunities to practice a new concept by repeating it in a playful context over and over again until it is securely embedded in the mind. The spontaneity that play offers is crucial in allowing children the freedom to experiment and explore both with materials and with role-play situations. This freedom allows for mistakes to be made in the process of 'coming to know' without the associated failure often attached to more formal learning styles. Play enables children to progress through all the stages of learning a concept, from first-hand experiences with the associated spoken language to symbolic play which involves the integration of all that a child knows, feels and can do.

This latter type of play, often called 'free-flow play', is a high level of learning activity. As the EYFS reminds us, 'In their play children learn at their highest level'.[42]

Play also helps children in their move away from egocentricity as they take on the roles of others and begin to experience life from a different perspective. It is through play such as this that children learn how it feels to be a mummy, a train driver or a shopkeeper as well as experiencing being part of a cooperative play scenario with all the turn-taking and negotiations involved in this type of play.

3

Children's physical and motor development

The EYFS requires practitioners to encourage the development of children's 'co-ordination, control, manipulation and movement' skills and to be 'active and interactive'. They must be 'supported in using all their senses' and begin to understand the importance of 'physical activity for health'. Alongside this, they need to be helped to 'make healthy choices in relation to food'.[43] This chapter will look at these areas, together with the theory that underpins both these requirements and the ways in which young children's bodies usually develop.

Body and mind are interlinked

Although in recent years, much research on children's development has focused on the functioning of the brain, it must be remembered that brain and body are, of course, inextricably linked. As Nurse states, 'The brain is fed by the information that the body submits to it'.[44] The function of the brain is to interpret this information that, particularly in the very young child, comes to it in the form of sensory experiences and emotions. This leads us to suppose that development is fundamentally affected by what happens to a child and does not occur by chance. This in turn means that the emotional and physical experiences that children have are of crucial importance in helping them to discover their bodies and their surroundings and to gain understandings of such fundamental concepts as time and space.

Helen Bee (1997) states other reasons for the study of physical and motor development in children. These are concerned with children's altered physical abilities, their increasing experience, the response that others have which alter as children grow and children's self-concept which is affected by physical changes. As well as enabling them to explore all aspects of their environment, successful physical development leads to new skills. Jennie Lindon expands this idea by stating that development in this area is not just 'more of the same' but a continual refinement of abilities.[45] This might be greater fine gripping and proficient manipulation of small objects plus ever-increasing strength and reach, which enables a wider (and usually higher) range of experimentation. These increasingly complex skills keep pace with children's insatiable appetite for discovery and exploration. An example of this might be the 3 years old who has received a scooter for her birthday. Just at the point when she has spurned her pushchair and exclaims, often forcibly, that she wants to run, she is given a gift that challenges her skills of balance yet offers her speed and independence. Much practice will be needed and there will be many a tumble before competence is achieved, especially that of operating the brake with the heel, but when success is achieved the sense of delight and resultant high levels of self-esteem are clear for all to see!

Physical prowess and mental health

Bee suggests that the increase in competence across a range of physical dimensions profoundly alters not only how the child perceives herself but, in turn, how the adults perceive, and consequently behave towards, the child. People will respond differently to a toddler who is still unsteady on his feet than to an older child who is managing to ride a bike with stabilisers. Although this sounds obvious, it is this reaction to progress and its attendant rise in expectations that drives the child to become ever more skilful. The relationship with the key adult here is vital in ensuring that success is encouraged and maintained.

In this way we can see that physical development and its attendant refinement of motor skills is inter-related to children's emotional and cognitive development. Children need interesting things to explore and discover to satisfy their urge of curiosity. This is what has made the treasure basket such a powerful tool in early years' settings, as it offers young babies choices about what to explore and in this way gives them a measure of self-determination and independence. The cognitive satisfaction of feeling and tasting a new object is matched by a positive emotional reaction in response to the pride shown by the carer in the baby's ability to reach for and explore an object in the basket. Once the key person's attitude towards this exploration is learned by the child, they will be confident enough of approval to try to discover what is further afield. Conversely, the child who spends long periods of time inactively in their pushchair or in front of the television does not receive these positive and encouraging responses to physical exploration and the curiosity drive may become dampened down. Robinson warns that we may 'underestimate the excitement of exploration for the child, with its resultant activation of reward and emotional systems in the brain'.[46] She states that neurochemical activity in the brain is triggered by the innate human drives of investigation and curiosity. As practitioners and carers, we must be mindful of how powerful an influence we are in our attitudes and in our provision as forces for the encouragement or suppression of this fundamental developmental drive. It may be, for example, very tempting for adults to remove reachable objects from the newly crawling toddler and to say 'No' as they approach a desired object, especially if it is the sound-stereo system! However, some thought needs to be given to the negative message that this will send to the child who is rightly proud of his new mobility skills! Clearly, unsafe and valuable items need to be protected but it is also important to praise and encourage the achievements and to replace precious items with those that are intriguing but safe.

27

In an article in *Nursery World*, Sally Goddard Blythe states that 'the foundation for learning is the physical readiness nurtured by carers in the years before a child starts school'.[47] In discussing why early movement experience matters, her findings from research suggest that, 'Sensations derived from exercising the balance mechanism help to train centres in the brain which are involved in the control of eye movements that will be necessary for reading, writing, copying and physical education, later on'.[48] Here we have some evidence that not only does physical exercise strengthen bodies and widen the range of possible movements but also it actually helps the young child to prepare for the fine motor skills required in reading and writing later on. Sadly, we currently read articles in newspapers[49] of schools forbidding children's games that involve running, in case of injury. A knowledge of child development by those making these decisions would be helpful, as they are possibly responsible for limiting the vital physical experiences that children need at a time when there is already deep concern about literary skills, in particular, writing, and especially boys' writing.

The specific physical skills that are thought to be needed to ensure a healthy body and a healthy mind have been identified by Goddard Blythe as *Attention*, *Balance* and *Co-ordination*, sometimes known as the ABC of learning success.[50] It is suggested here that not only children's physical and academic skills depend on proficiency in these three areas but also their resilience to later stress and anxiety.

'The ABC of learning success'

Learning actively

Young children are not usually reluctant to develop their physical skills. They delight in clambering, jumping, rolling and running at every opportunity! It is as if they are hard-wired to extend their physical expertise and by doing so lay the foundations for all other types of successful learning and development. Jerome Bruner remarked that movement and action represent the 'culture of childhood'[51] and this echoes the work of Jean Piaget, whose fundamental influence on early years of education concerned his assertion that children are agents in their own learning and that they construct their own meanings as a result of interacting with the environment.

The idea of active learning is central to another of Piaget's theories – that of schemes of thought or schemas. Just as adults may need external props such as maps or lists to complete a task or a journey, so young children need to practice concepts that they are learning. Children can become very determined as they repeatedly play in specific ways, resistant to adult requests to modify their play and unable to explain why they are playing in this almost obsessive way. Concepts that are often explored in this way are trajectories, or 'up and down, to and fro movements', enclosing, transportation, connections and circles. Consider the following example.

In one nursery, 4-year-old Zoe spent as much time as possible in each session clambering underneath tables and then emerging for just enough time to collect a doll from the role-play area before disappearing once more underneath a piece of furniture. When staff talked to her she could only say that she liked 'being inside and under things'. Staff realised that Zoe was finding out what the concepts of 'in' and 'out' felt like and sugested that she might like to try making a house in the workshop for her doll. Zoe then enjoyed playing in the tent in the nursery garden and often drew pictures that featured houses, tents and boxes. Her schema was helping her learn about the concept of 'in and out'. There is a more detailed analysis of children's schematic learning in Cathy Nutbrown's book *Threads of Thinking*.[52] Schematic play is, then, an essentially active exploration of basic concepts and, as a process, is extremely effective in securing embedded understanding in the child's brain. As children continue to learn ever-more complex ideas in this way, they gain ever more control over their environment, which progressively makes more sense to them. Schematic play is a perfect example of cognition, motivation and physical development working in harmony. As a concept becomes securely understood and is lodged in the brain, the child becomes less dependent on repeating the schematic behaviour and the play will come to a natural end. It is rather like driving a car or playing a musical instrument; once learned, these basic actions and understandings become automatic, thus freeing up the brain to operate at a higher level and concentrate on, for example, road traffic conditions or expressions of emotion and technique in the music. The way that schematic behaviours can be catered for in different areas of provision will become apparent in the following chapters.

The process of learning actively is clearly visible in the child who starts to play with an unknown object: a Sellotape dispenser perhaps. At first the child thinks 'What is this?' and watches others, touches it and thinks about it until a possible purpose becomes apparent. The child moves on to begin to take control over the dispenser by thinking 'What can I do with it?' A lot of time has to be spent mastering its complexities before the child can use it with mastery and begin to make 'creations'. At this point, the child is thinking *'How can I use this to play my way?'* By this time, physical dexterity has had to be well developed and only consistent practice with support from an interested companion can put these sets of skills in place to enable competence at this level. This idea of progressive learning can provide a useful basis for planning the equipment for an area of provision, and in thinking about how it will be staffed. The adult team need to ensure that provision for a full range of abilities is met, both for those children with delayed development and those who are new to the setting, as well as for those with a high level of physical coordination and dexterity.

Learning through the senses

The earliest information that comes to a baby is through the senses. It is thought that the sense of smell is the first to be in place after birth and the last to go at death. Certainly, scents can act as powerful triggers of past experiences or even times of the year. The smell of cinnamon and cloves is often linked to Christmas and the smell of freshly baked bread can only too easily suggest hunger! Children need to be attuned to smells by having their attention drawn to the particular smells of everyday objects such as flowers and cooking ingredients. In this way they are not only developing their olfactory abilities but also becoming cognitively more adept at discrimination and identification. An approach that is often used in working with young children is known as VAK and concentrates on visual, auditory and kinaesthetic learning. Although this approach does not cover all the senses, it provides a good starting point when considering both what to provide for young children to experience physically and also what their individual learning styles might be. Many a young child who may not appear to shine academically may be skilled with a football or a paintbrush and these artistic and dextrous learners need to know that their abilities are valued as highly as are numerical and literary ones.

Teaching children to look carefully is one of the most important skills we can help them acquire. Children absorb much information visually, often from the faces of those around them. The brain selects what information a child needs to know and this function serves as a filter so that children are attuned to pick up what visual information is important for them. Visual signals include the body language and facial expressions of key people and their peers, so that they can judge what might be an appropriate response. As natural observers, children can be encouraged to examine interesting objects such as clocks which tick, flowers which open or feathers that drift to the ground. They will thus develop a habit of learning which will stand them in very good stead all their lives: that of noticing how the world around them functions.

Visual images in the early years setting can provide a good support to auditory learning methods which tend to predominate. Children of around 4 or 5 can begin to visualise a model or project they are considering and can be encouraged, with help, to draw a plan. This helps them to embed their project firmly in their mind and, having a clearer picture, tends to lead to more persistence as the project or creation takes shape. An added commitment and realistic sense of sequence will often tip the balance in favour of success rather than a random, less focused outcome.

Photos of the children can supplant the familiar alphabet that is on most nursery walls and photos of how to follow simple recipes can teach not only cooking but also a sense of sequence. Many settings use photos very successfully to show what some of the possibilities are in an area of provision or to provide evidence of achievement for assessment. Photos and posters can underpin cultural and gender issues too by emphasising a range of midwinter festivals as well as Christmas or by showing pictures of female doctors and male care workers. The fact that these are displayed gives the values that are captured within these pictures a status that defines the principles of the setting as well as making suggestions to children.

Children with visual impairment will often have an acute sense of hearing or will have refined another sense, such as touch, in the place of, or alongside, vision. Practitioners will need to be aware of their children's particular needs and ensure that, when concentrating on a sensory experience, each child can partake in ways that are satisfying to them.

Learning through the sense of hearing has become rather a fraught area in current times. A child's world is so full of noise, much of it background noise, that it can be hard to help children develop auditory discrimination. Where as children are able to 'switch off' much background sound, it is then harder for them to learn to listen to sounds that are important. This has a knock-on effect with speech, as children need to be able to hear and then replicate the nuances of the spoken word to be effectively understood. Auditory games in settings, such as clapping a repeated rhythm and clapping 'question and answer' activities, will help children practice the art of listening, which they will need when engaging in conversations.

The sense of touch is yet another tricky area. Teaching young children about touch cannot realistically be limited to a feely bag with scratchy and silky pieces of material inside. Young children need both to gain security by receiving affectionate and genuine comfort and reassurance when it is needed. They also need to learn what an appropriate and responsive touch between children and adults is like. Physical contact is intertwined with emotional well-being, as we considered in Chapter 1, and has profound implications for children's emotional literacy as well as their academic achievement. It is entirely possible for a setting to reflect confidence in a philosophy which might be called 'professional intimacy', where children and adults alike are clear about the boundaries of relationships and physical contact. The word 'intimacy' in this context means that the adults love their key children and enjoy their company. They are excited by their achievements and supportive in their endeavours. There will be smiles, a guiding hand on the shoulder and cuddles on laps in cases of distress; but the key word here is 'professional' and the child's trust in the adult derives from this professionalism. Within these boundaries, it is entirely possible for key people, who are trusted by children and their families, to offer the emotional care that children need to thrive. These ideas about the key person as an emotional relationship are expanded by Elfer, Goldschmeid, and Sellick, in their book 'Key Persons in the Nursery'.[53]

The role of the adult

To help children develop physical and motor skills and to develop an awareness of all their senses, the adult team's approach needs to be two-fold: first, there needs to be an environment which supports this development by being interesting and challenging; secondly, adults need to allocate time to teaching children specific skills which will help them gain proficiency in using the tools and equipment they need to be creative and expressive. These two aspects will work best if given equal importance, so that the child who has spotted the weaving activity knows that if he approaches it, an adult will be available to help him with the fine motor skills of coordination that he needs to achieve the task. Conversely, there are many settings which, in undervaluing children's physical development and underestimating their potential, have provided outside areas which are totally paved in soft surface tarmac and contain nothing more physically challenging or interesting than indoor toys which have been brought outside. There may be less need here for adults to engage in teaching time-consuming skills of 'co-ordination, control, manipulation and movement' or to help children as they practice the often unpredictable business of being 'active and interactive',[54] but, as educators, we are failing children if we do not give them these opportunities and support them while they learn what are, after all, skills for life.

Planning must include opportunities for children to develop their gross motor skills, which include running, jumping, throwing and catching, hopping, climbing, crawling and rolling. This is all much easier to provide in the outside area, as we have seen in Chapter 5, though some of these activities can transfer indoors with a little imagination. Children will need to be taught to use tools such as glue, scissors and staplers and, once taught and given consistent opportunities to use them, will have progressively fewer accidents. A key feature of successful tool use in young children is to allow as much access as possible. Allowing the woodwork only on a fine afternoon when extra staffing is available will not result in children able to manipulate drills, hammers and saws with any competence and although there are often hard choices to be made in terms of staffing and equipment, an audit of the setting's priorities should, be made in the interests of a child's development. So it is important to put activities such as woodwork, weaving, sewing, model making and drawing at the top of the agenda. Activities such as these have an intrinsic delight for the child, add greatly to their image of self-worth and contribute significantly to their abilities to observe, concentrate, manipulate, sequence and later, to read and to write.

The role of play in physical and motor development

Following from the EYFS theme of Learning and Developing, cards 4.1, 4.2 and 4.3 are explicit about the active nature of children's learning and development. In particular, card 4.1 gives specific guidance regarding the contexts in which children will develop most successfully. As well as this, the cards state that 'children need plenty of space and time to play both outdoors and indoors'. They need 'dens and dressing-up' and opportunities to playfully practice with equipment before being asked to use it to produce completed projects or 'solve problems'. As we saw in the instance of the Sellotape dispenser in the section on Learning Actively, above, children need to be able to spend a lot of time freely trying things out in ways of their choosing. In using trial and error, they become ever closer to dexterity, agility, competence and independence. As we shall see in the chapter on creativity, this process involves mess and a heavy use of resources without necessarily providing much to show in terms of tangible results but is nonetheless a crucial part of the process of becoming competent.

What and how children play is dependent on what is available. The EYFS has a theme devoted to 'enabling environments'; indeed, the environment is often referred to as 'the third teacher', (parents and carers being the first two). In her article 'The Environment as the third Teacher',[55] Darragh draws on the work of Urie Bronfenbreener to suggest that the environment will support children's play and learning because it is dynamic. In other words, a child's relationship with the environment is a reciprocal process. The child will impact on the environment and the environment will impact on the child. By throwing his ball onto the floor, the little boy in his pushchair, whom we have already considered, is able to practice what he is beginning to know about gravity. He needs the environment to help him learn about these new ideas. It follows, therefore, that the setting's environment has to be rich to support learning in this way. The outside area we thought of earlier, with its safe surface and little challenge, will be less dynamic and offer less learning to the curious child. There will be less to be curious about, less to interact with and so, in turn, less will be learned.

For resources to support play in this dynamic and interactive way, the adult team will need to ask themselves some key questions:

- Are there enough resources for the number of children you anticipate using them?
- Are they fit for purpose: i.e. in good condition?
- How will the children be able to use resources? Will it be for their own purposes or for those of the adults?
- What are the time and space constraints on the use of resources?
- Is there support for children's schematic play?
- Do resources support children at different stages of development, of both genders, and do they reflect children's rights to equality and their diversity?
- Do resources focus on children's thinking and actions rather than on a completed project or end product?
- Are staffs deployed flexibly to enable enough support to be offered to children using new or challenging resources?

Some of these questions refer not to the resources themselves but to the ways in which they are used. It is this aspect which is most important in ensuring children's effective development, not only of their physical and motor skills but also in all areas. It is the emotional environment, EYFS Card 3.3, which impacts most powerfully on how children's development progresses. As this card goes on to explain, it is in the warm and accepting philosophy of an empathetic and loving environment where children understand that they are accepted and valued that they will have the most courage to extend their developmental boundaries by trying things out.

Here they will be safe in the knowledge that failure is all part of the process of learning and that in the uncertain business of gaining new skills, practitioners are alongside them, supporting their endeavours and celebrating their successes.

Children's social and language development

In this book the decision was taken to consider children's social and language development together. This is because, in reality, they do develop together. They are intertwined and inter-dependent so that children can access to what they need to survive. Survival and progress depend to a very large extent on children's ability to communicate successfully with those adults and peers who are in a position to satisfy their physical, emotional and cognitive needs. Communication usually takes the form of spoken language but in a child who has no language because of physical or other forms of disability, different communication systems such as signing and touch are powerful enough to satisfy a young child's needs.[56] What is important here is that the emphasis is on *language* rather than *speech*. There can be many ways of communicating, of which speech is by far the most usual, but others are just as effective in establishing powerful communication. The EYFS, Card 1.1 tells us that the young child is 'a skilful communicator'. This use of the word 'skilful' reminds us once again that the baby and very young child are not lacking in intelligence – all they lack is experience.

Interactive learning

The main way in which children acquire language is by communicating with someone they trust and who they know loves them. Research tells us that we should adopt a healthy scepticism of all the merchandise currently available that claims to help a baby or young child develop more quickly than they are designed to do. 'Everything we know about babies suggests that these artificial inventions are at best useless and at worst distractions from the normal interaction between grown-ups and babies'.[57] We know that the developing brain of the young child has synapses that make new connections when children are introduced to a new idea that intrigues them and when their curiosity is aroused. What then enables them to learn about this new idea and the language that accompanies it is the trusted adult who is present, responding to the child's interest and sharing the discovery. Thus, we come back to the toddler in the pushchair, that we considered in the chapter on cognitive and intellectual development, who was enjoying watching his ball rolling away. The adult picks up the ball, returns it to the child and says something like 'Is this your ball, then?' The toddler learns several very important things: first, the concept that a round object rolls; secondly, that it has a name, '*ball*'; and thirdly, that this is an enjoyable interaction which can be repeated many times! In this simple example of everyday experiences, one can see that the child is developing cognitively (*the ball rolls*), linguistically (*it has a name*), socially (*this is a fun interaction*) and emotionally (*this type of interaction only happens with people who are important and consistent carers*). It is in just this type of everyday interaction that young children learn their first words; they are nouns or 'naming words'. We can see from this example that children progress in several different aspects of their development all at the same time because of the interaction involved. It is the interaction that is the 'glue' that makes the other aspects of the learning come together as a holistic learning experience. This depth of learning would not be gained from television programmes or computer games even if they had a specific language focus and were designed to teach language. The vital component that is missing from these programmes and games is the interactive one, which, as we have seen, is the most powerful. When we talk, we accompany the spoken word with gestures, expressions and many other clues to help the listener make sense of what is meant by the words that are being spoken. A baby will be able to understand much more than they can say because they know the people who talk to them intimately and will be able to interpret the context of the talk – i.e. what is meant – by the accompanying tones and gestures. This interpretation is not possible through the medium of the computer or the television screen, partly because the presenters are not known, loved and trusted by the children watching. As this is being written, research has been published by Jean Gross, the 'communication champion', which takes up and debates just this point.[58]

The first language

Children usually begin to acquire spoken language as they approach their first birthday but, as in all other forms of learning, much practice has to take place first! The babbling that a baby does is just that: learning what talking sounds like and practising making the noises that will form the words that they will need to communicate effectively. Their first recognisable word is often 'Mama' or a variation of what they call their mother. This may be because it is a straightforward sound to make, but possibly because it is the word they need to connect with the person who means most to them. The language that is used to talk to a baby is often called 'motherese', or, more accurately perhaps, 'infant-directed speech', and is designed to emphasis high and low notes that a baby can easily distinguish. It is also spoken at close range to the baby's face and is accompanied by exaggerated facial expressions. This all emphasises the meaning of the words and helps the baby enormously as the baby can extract the meaning from body language and facial expressions long before spoken language is acquired. In fact, body language remains key in our communications with others even when we, as adults, are skilled linguistically.

'A child's social development is central to their ability to function fully as a successful human being'. In their work on socialisation, Lynne Murray and Liz Andrews show very young babies both responding to the actions and body language of their carers and initiating social interactions.[59]

As practitioners, our body language is vital in communicating to our key children how we feel about them and we will consider later in this section what professional attitudes we convey to our children, colleagues and parents by how we look and present ourselves. Children are skilled at interpreting our body language as they have been practising since they were born!

Rosemary Roberts confirms this by stating that 'How we look, and the way in which something is said, is likely to mean more to a young child than the words themselves'.[60] We need to acknowledge that communication, of any sort, is a two-way process and be aware that our responses to our key children will be expertly interpreted by them and will reflect our feelings towards them.

Learning spoken language

The brain is so constructed as to enable any language to be learned up until around the first birthday. At that point the young child becomes exclusively attuned to the language of its culture so that the predominant language that is heard tends to be the one that is learned. Children are able to learn two, or even more, languages when they are very young because of this flexibility of the brain's language acquisition function at the start of life.

The process of language acquisition is complex and is debated in great depth elsewhere in the literature of early education, by amongst others, Vygotsky,[61] Wells[62] and Pinker.[63] The purpose of this chapter is to consider what the implications of the research we read may have for us as educators of those children who are in the midst of the process of acquiring spoken language. One of the major implications is that to acquire effective spoken language children need to be in sociable situations where they have real reasons and opportunities to talk, to listen and to begin to engage in that complex business of having a conversation. To hold a conversation a child needs not only to be able to talk and to listen but also to be able to alternate these twin skills with a sense of empathy, to question and to be responsive to the other person's spoken ideas, suggestions and commands. They then begin to share their own imaginative ideas, become assertive to ensure that their needs are met and to start contributing to a group discussion.

In the early stages of language acquisition most children seem to centre on the business of classification; i.e. by asking 'What name does this object have?' Classification in itself is a complex skill to acquire. Take, as an example, this conversation between Albert, aged 2, and his grandmother:

Grandmother: 'Look at that big black and white bird, Albert'.
Albert: 'That not bird, that magpie'.

In this exchange, Albert is not trying to impress his grandmother by his wide knowledge of birds but he is muddled. His father has told him that the large black and white

'They then begin to share their own imaginative ideas'

object is a magpie but his grandmother is giving it a different name. He is not yet experienced enough to understand that an object can be both a bird and a magpie. His classification skills are at an early stage and he will yet have to master such complexities as, for example, two cows and four sheep equalling six animals! The young child's language acquisition is driven by the 'need to know', and to have these needs met and by individual, gender, and cultural interests. The child, for example, from a family who are knowledge-able about insects will, from a very young age, be able to distinguish a worm from an earwig and be able to name them. Many very young boys are knowledgeable about the similarities and differences between various types of machinery spotted on building sites!

Some children develop language in a rather different way. Helen Bee suggests although many children have a 'referential style' of learning to talk: i.e., they learn classification as a first step. Some children adopt what she refers to as an 'expressive style', which involves the use of more personal words connected with the emotions.[64] These words may include 'Yes', 'No', 'You' and 'Me' and then develop into short empathetic phrases such as 'Love you' or 'Go away'. No research has yet found a defin-itive reason for this variation, but for us, as educators, the two factor that underlie all successful language acquisition, whichever style is used, are the trusted companion and the stimulating environment. The environment in which the young child is learning to talk is the overriding determinant of success, even though neuroscience tells us that humans are born with a predisposition to tune into spoken language. We will come back to the business of providing a rich language environment later on.

The building of self-image

The child who acquires a rich vocabulary is one who is secure in their relationship with their key people. As language is acquired through social interaction, it is vital that the child has a self-concept which is positive. This positive view will give the child the courage to experiment with words, try out their ideas on someone else and become assertive within the family and their setting or school community and to be able to accept disagreement or non-comprehension. The successful child needs to know that they will be listened to and needs to believe that they have interesting things to say. This concept will have been building from the very earliest days of life and is sometimes called the 'mirroring process'.

Thus, the young child's social development can be thought of through several 'aspects', the first of which is:

Perception of self. This is the area of development which involves the mirroring process, where the child reflects on what has been experienced. Where the child receives smiles, encouragement and stimulation, there will be a reflected positive self-image.

Relationships with others. The child who has received a positive response to their personality, abilities and ideas, and thereby has developed a positive self-image, will meet other children with confidence and enthusiasm. This child will also have begun to learn about actions and their consequences and to understand about tolerance and sensitivity. These 'empathetic' skills are only learned through a range of interactions.

Response to the environment. This aspect of social learning centres on how feelings, ideas and experiences are represented. Here the child learns that both ordinary and extraordinary events can be replayed again and again through role play, dance, painting, small-world play and music. The child also learns about appropriate emotional responses to events; that it is right to feel sad when an important person leaves and that emotions such as anger and excitement are often appropriate too. We shall consider later in this chapter about how these emotions can be catered for in the setting and, indeed, can provide valuable learning experiences.

All of these aspects of social development have a common feature running through them and that is *time*. Confident children with a good self-image will have had much time invested in them by parents, carers and their 'important people'.

It takes time to be responsive to a child's uncertain early utterances, to show how important we think these are and to demonstrate that we genuinely enjoy their company.

It is those children who have experienced an unhurried and gentle response to their efforts who will have the confidence to try out new words and phrases. In the course of the busy lives that most of us lead, time is a precious commodity. Nowhere, I would like to suggest, can time be more usefully invested than with the young child learning not only new words but also what kind of person they are perceived to be. The early years setting has some advantages over the home in that iPods and televisions are not likely to be taking the attention of the adult away from the talking child or vice versa. Interestingly, though, it is in the home that the child has more opportunities to *ask* questions rather than *answer* them. In their research into the quality of working class girls' spoken language, Barbara Tizzard and Martin Hughes found that it was in the home, rather than in school, that spoken language was more richly developed, because parents responded to children's questions as opposed to expecting the child to respond to adult questioning.[65] What we understand about the process of learning tells us that intrinsic motivation is a powerful driver: i.e. when we want to know something our interest is more likely to be sustained. Imagine, for example, arriving at a self-chosen evening class in watercolour painting only to discover that it has been changed to a class in car maintenance. This is so far distanced from the original choice as to make the switch almost impossible and the likelihood is that the class would not be attended by those hoping to learn how to paint! Yet, we do a similar thing to children when we ask them questions to which we need the answers, but hold little interest for them. Questions often heard in settings such as, '*How many counters can you see?*' or '*Is the pot half full or is it empty?*', are, in truth, more about assessment than about teaching new knowledge by following a child's interests. Children can perhaps be forgiven for offering a low-level, single-word response or even none at all. This type of interaction will not encourage children's language development and is a million miles from the 'sustained shared thinking' that was highlighted in the EPPE[66] report as being a key feature of children's successful learning. The wise practitioner will recognise this pitfall and be careful to structure any necessary questions so that the child is able to retain an equal share of the conversation and is thus motivated to continue thinking, listening and talking.

Children, in a school situation, often feel inhibited and, unless responsive situations are in place to support their emergent skills, will often not feel confident enough to try them out. Children will talk most freely:

- to a trusted adult
- to another child
- within a known group
- when they feel they have a worthwhile contribution to make
- when they are initiating activities.

The language environment

Having established that young children's literacy development thrives in an atmosphere of trust and rich experiences, the practitioner is in a good position to ensure that the setting provides these necessities. By observing children carefully, practitioners can discover what triggers their interest and when they are most likely talk freely and with confidence and enthusiasm. One basic requirement is that there must be interesting things to talk about! A setting where children are restricted by many safety requirements may find that, in removing all risk, many of the challenges and curiosities that encourage children to talk to each other about what they are discovering have also been removed. Consider the following example:

> Rashid and Humzah are in the outside sandpit with the outdoor wooden bricks. They want to build a castle with the bricks and are trying to gauge the consistency of the sand, to which, by adding water, they hope to make 'cement' that will glue the bricks together. They discuss the project, start mixing their cement and occasionally decide that more water is needed. 'You get the water, then I'll get the water, then you get the water', Rasheed suggests as he dictates the sharing of responsibilities. 'That's too much' says Humzah as the water begins to wash away the sand: 'Tip some away'. The co-operation continues until they have agreed on the right consistency and start to build the walls of their castle, adding generous amounts of cement between the bricks. The conversation progresses to debate the height of the walls, which are being built to protect the castle and how dinosaurs and dragons can be kept outside! This everyday project encourages conversations for real reasons, it enables genuine cooperation and allows the two friends to initiate an activity and to think deeply about both the practicalities and the imaginative aspects of their project. It is a rich learning experience for both boys. Had the setting decided that perhaps this activity would be rather too messy, or take too long, or that the bricks could not be used with the sand, the whole richness of this learning experience would have been lost.

If a prime requirement to encourage talking and listening is to have interesting things to talk about, another is that there should be plenty of time for projects such as these to develop. Rich, thoughtful and complex conversations such as these cannot flourish in a few minutes only; they need time, and possibly nurturing by an interested practitioner who might ask how the project is going and enquire if children need any help or additional materials. There is a fine dividing line, of course, between interacting and interfering and only lots of experience will help the practitioner get it right most of the time!

Another requirement that is needed for genuine conversations to flourish is that children should understand that what they do and say will be valued and respected. If a setting's expectation is that conversations with children will be mainly managerial – for example, *'Put your painting on the shelf to dry'* – there are few opportunities for rich interactions to develop.

If, on the other hand, a practitioner asks *'Which colour did you paint first?',* this type of interaction sends a clear message to the child that the adult is interested in the work done and values it enough to ask questions about it. A conversation can easily open up from this point and there is the added advantage that the child is being asked to think more deeply about the work produced. This reinforces the learning by making the child remember what they did. There is also the expectation in this kind of exchange that children are to be a little thoughtful and perhaps reflective, thus raising the level of the child's commitment to their activities. A further requirement in the setting is that there is someone special to the child who is responsive and enthusiastic to their creations. A very young child will only feel confident to discuss their project with someone who is trusted and it is important to them that this is the person who is on hand to participate in the conversation about the child's work.

Talking and listening needs to be planned for every area of the setting. Practitioners need to consider which features about a planned activity or area of provision are those that will encourage children to talk and listen, either to other children or to an adult. A role-play area such as a train station, for example, needs to incorporate a ticket office where children say where they are going, and buy a ticket. A hairdresser's shop needs to encourage conversations about hairstyles and costs, while a garage could have mechanics who ask what needs fixing with the vehicles that have been brought in. Adults may need to model these conversations at first but, once familiar with the routines, children will have no shortage of imaginative ideas.

Art areas and workshop areas also provide rich opportunities for conversations about processes such as how to mix the paint to get the colour just right or how to get two pieces of paper to stick together. Once children understand that spoken language is such a useful tool, they will gain confidence in using it for a range of purposes, from getting what they need (finding more glue, perhaps) as well as furthering their idea (by engaging in a 'let's pretend' game).

Developing social skills

For young children to develop good social skills, or what is sometimes known as prosocial behaviour, they need to feel good about themselves and to feel a certain amount of autonomy and independence. As we have seen earlier, it is much easier for children to 'form good relationships with adults and peers'[67] if they are secure in the knowledge that their own emotional and material needs are being met. At the very heart of their social confidence in the setting is understanding that they, individually, belong to their group, that they are an equal member of it and that what they say and do is important. It will be noted that good social skills was one of the three 'super skills' of learning discussed in the Startright Report,[68] which we considered in Chapter 1. Possession of these skills is based on a combination of personality and experience and they consist of being able to appreciate how others are feeling (often called empathy), and to have the well-being of others at heart (often called altruism). The EYFS requires the 5-year-old child to 'understand what is right, what is wrong and why'[69] to achieve the early learning goal in this area and, yet, for children to meet this requirement fully, a range of understandings about what is acceptable behaviour in a particular place as well as positive feelings about themselves and others need to be in place before 'what is right' and 'what is *wrong'* can be identified. As an adult, it is often very hard to distinguish right from wrong and even more difficult to understand why. For the young child, still egocentric and still new to adult perceptions of morality, a realistic assessment of what is the right course of action is often a step too far. It is an unrealistic expectation, for example, to ask a young child to *'share nicely'* when, from the child's perspective, a developmental lack of empathy leads her to take the brick she needs to complete her building from a nearby child who has just used it for a similar purpose. Maria Robinson[70] suggests that humans have a deep sense of territory which is evolutionary and linked to elemental feelings of safety. Placing large numbers of young children closely together with insufficient space and things to play with is not conducive to pro-social behaviour as they struggle to ensure their needs are met. As Jennie Lindon so expressively puts it (*Understanding Child Development*), 'He who shoves, gets'.[71]

In the early years setting, it is often with the adults that the work of implementing a positive social environment begins. Adults need to be trained to model the behaviour they expect from children and to appreciate that time spent in teaching children what is acceptable and what is not is time well spent. They may also need help to understand that conflict is sometimes the result of routines and organisations that encourage aggressive behaviour. Occasions, for example, when children have to wait for long periods of time with nothing to do or areas of the setting which have insufficient equipment are often trigger points for exasperation. Careful observations of conflict points and of children who have particular difficulties will give evidence of what is going wrong and provide a starting point for a remedy. Some children, for example, find joining a group of playing children challenging or some may find the outside area a hard place in which to remain calm. The teacher or manager who is leading the practice has a clear role here in identifying difficult times and places and suggesting solutions. A possible solution is to teach children the words and phrases they need to ensure that their needs are met; phrases such as *'I haven't finished with it yet'* have prevented many a shove! In fact, those children with the most highly developed linguistic skills are those who can be most acceptably assertive and who, in consequence, feel most independent and self-confident.

How can play support children's social and language development?

Imaginative play is the ideal vehicle for children to practice their developing linguistic and social skills in a safe way. Children are, in fact, often seen playing 'naughty children' or 'stern teachers', displaying behaviour that is certainly not pro-social, but completely acceptable as it is 'play'. *'But we are only playing'*, children will often remind themselves and any nearby adult who is questioning the increasingly violent script!

As well as role play, there are other types of play where practice in the fields of both language and social behaviour are possible. Word games, nursery rhymes and songs help children to develop their skills in spoken language and they often delight in making up rhymes and imaginary words.

The adult has many roles in encouraging pro-social behaviour in children's play. They may be the facilitator who ensures that children have all that they need for their play. They may intervene to suggest how the play may be extended and therefore more satisfying to the players or they may mediate in a dispute. Through these roles the adult is seen by the children as a positive influence, a resource to whom they may turn and a trusted companion who leads their thinking towards positive behaviour, empathy and altruism.

Section 2 Areas of learning in the setting

The outdoors

Allow sufficient space, indoors and outdoors, to set up relevant activities for energetic play.[72]

One of the major joys that young children have is to be surrounded by enough space to be really energetic, to explore to the limits their physical skills and to thus gain the confidence to 'take manageable risks in their play'.[73] In this chapter we will explore how this valuable area of provision can give children opportunities to develop not only their physical skills but also to develop emotionally, socially and cognitively. In other words, a well-resourced outside area is a rich environment, offering learning opportunities across the curriculum. Through play there are possibilities for children to experience a wide range of areas of enquiry – mathematical, scientific and technological, creative and linguistic – in enjoyable and independent ways which we considered in greater depths in Chapter 1.

It could be argued that the area of children's physical development has been the one area most at risk over the last 30 years. The work of the early years pioneers such as Margaret McMillan and Susan Isaacs, who founded their curriculum on the value of the outdoors, has been forced into the background as value has been placed on different models and styles of learning. The emphasis on academic bodies of knowledge and formal learning styles has influenced the early years curriculum and narrowed it to exclude some of its most precious elements. Some voices have continued to fight for balance and worked hard to uphold the values of physical development and outdoor learning by continuing to assert that it is central to high-quality early years practice. These educators, such as Margaret Edgington, Marjorie Ouvrey and Helen Bilton, have been successful in raising the status of outdoor learning and the work of the Forests Schools has developed these ideas, helping to lessen the impact of today's curtailment of the outdoors with their resultant problems of obesity, lack of social skills and empathy with the environment. The EYFS Practice Guidance (p 7) requires settings to 'provide opportunities for children to play indoors and outdoors'[74] and yet, all too often, the outdoors is seen as a replica of the inside with unchallenging equipment and compliant children. Children often do not have the opportunities to learn through those experiences which are unique to the outside because of the risk they are perceived to pose to health and safety.

This chapter is based on the understanding that the outdoors is an outdoor classroom. This means that the same expectations of learning and behaviour apply outside as inside and that the outside is planned for in the same way as the inside. It is not an area where children go to 'let off steam', as this implies that they are being constrained by formal learning indoors from which they need to escape. Not an appropriate philosophy for the Foundation Stage! The outdoor area, as a learning environment, has been under threat since the 1980s when an emphasis was placed on the value of cognitive development over and above other areas of development. With this shift in emphasis, the more 'measurable' and (sic) valuable learning was thought to happen indoors, thus confirming the opinion that the outdoors was not productive in terms of learning new knowledge, concepts and skills. Of course, this becomes a self-fulfilling prophecy. If time in the garden is restricted and it is poorly resourced and unwillingly supervised by staff who do not understand its value, the play becomes frantic and children have no time or enough rich resources to extend and develop their learning. The quality of their experiences are consequently of a low level and everyone is confirmed in their view that being outside is a poor use of everyone's time.

The following description is that of a large, multi-sensory environment to which children have access for much of their time at the setting. The flexible use of equipment and materials reflects the staff's understanding of the principle: 'Children learn best when they are given appropriate responsibility, allowed to experiment, make errors, decisions and choices, and are respected as autonomous learners'[75]. Of course, not everyone can have the 'garden of their dreams' but it is nevertheless possible to plan an area that is distinct in its nature from the inside and is a place where children can learn things that can only be experienced outside: for example, how things grow, digging, the weather and working with messy and large-scale activities.

The example that follows is not perfect, but does provide for learning across the whole curriculum as well as experiences in most developmental areas. Practitioners will not necessarily have everything described here but may have some of it and may have different activities, such as woodwork, which will offer similar learning opportunities. Most settings may have to choose carefully the right amount and the right balance of equipment to suit the space available and this is often challenging. Too little to do will find children struggling to satisfy their curiosity and yet too much equipment will crowd the space so that quarrels ensue as children try to practice gross motor skills such as running, throwing and rolling that are most effectively learned outside.

A nursery garden

This garden is in an inner city nursery school. It has a small grassed area and a larger hard-surfaced area for wheeled toys. Most of the wheeled toys take two children, a driver and a passenger. There are evergreen flowering shrubs, a lilac tree, from which hang two bird feeders, and two digging areas. One digging area is for growing flowers and vegetables, whereas the other is for, well, just digging, to see what might be in the soil. There is an area which has a soft surface and on this stands a climbing frame. Set into the hard surface area is a large sand pit which is covered with a lightweight cover which is rolled across to protect it overnight. The soil which was dug out to make the sand pit has been grassed to make a small hill down which the children love to run and roll. There is a water tray on wheels that can be moved indoors if necessary and a quantity of plastic guttering that can be used in conjunction with the sand pit or the water trough. In a shed nearby is a range of smaller equipment that can be accessed easily by staff in accordance with current planning. There are wooden steps and ladders that attach to the climbing frame, large bricks and hoops to make an obstacle course. There is a small tent that is straightforward to erect and a few child-size tables and chairs than can be arranged to make a role-play area such as a garage, station or car park. In the shed are kept some prams, pushchairs and some 'outside dolls'. These dolls are allowed to be taken on adventures which might make them rather muddy, sandy or wet and so the children decided to have an inside set and an outside set! Also in the shed is an outdoor picnic set that can be used with the dolls, or in the outside role-play area or in the sand and water. There is a box of chalks and large rolls of paper and study crayons. A set of large wooden 'outside' bricks are stored here, too, and enable children to extend the role-play possibilities as they are invaluable as props in a wide range of make believe games. A conically shaped 'loom' made from bamboo canes and originally designed for supporting sweet peas, makes an open-ended weaving activity.

There are some stilts and some large and small balls and a basketball hoop attached to one wall. There is a plastic tunnel through which children can crawl and buckets with water and different-sized brushes for children to draw or write with water. There are games such as skittles and some light, plastic bats.

A hutch contains two guinea pigs (Bubble and Squeak) that are housed at the nursery and spend most days in a run attached to their hutch in the garden.

The garden is surrounded by a fence which has security locks at the gates and is easily accessible to the inside area. There is an outside tap which children can use and gardening equipment to help with the care of anything that is planted.

In Chapters 1-4 we considered the theory underpinning children's emotional, physical, social and cognitive development. So here we will take those aspects of development in turn and think about how they can be catered for in the outside area of the setting. We will also consider the associated practitioner questions.

Children's emotional and behavioural development

Self-esteem

Being outdoors has a positive impact in children's sense of well-being and helps all aspects of children's development.[76]

The outside area gives children unique opportunities that are not available indoors and often the most powerful early play experiences that adults recall are those that took place outside. Here, children's self-esteem can be given a real boost as they hone their skills to hop, throw, catch, balance and climb. How often does the early years practitioner hear the joyful shout 'Look what I can do!' from a 4 years old balancing along a low beam or scoring a goal for the first time? The growth in the child's self-esteem is significant and it is nearly always a physical milestone that delights the child to such an extent.

Conversely, for some children the outside area poses a number of challenges. Sometimes being in a slightly less constrained area removes familiar boundaries and adds a little uncertainty to an already less familiar environment where the expectations may seem rather more blurred than indoors. Children may spend a lot of time, especially at first, watching other children to see whether, for example, they are allowed to 'paint' the fence with water, whether they can climb into the guinea pigs' run and to discover where they can dig. Some children who have had little or no access to the outside may find the insects worrying rather than intriguing and will need help in experiencing and in observing them. The result of this may be that some children find they feel less confident about themselves outside, as it is a less predictable environment. The outside presents proportionately more opportunities to fall while climbing, to trip while running, to get muddy while digging and to be bumped by a passing tricycle.

In the garden described above, most children learned to climb the lilac tree before they left the nursery. This was not a challenge set by the adults, just a tradition that grew up amongst the children as they devised an ever wider range of routes to the next branch.

Here must be mentioned the everpresent concern about risks associated with learning. In her excellent book 'Too Safe for Their Own Good? Helping Children Learn about Risks and Lifeskills".[77] Jennie Lindon explores these issues in depth. Here it may be sufficient to say that, of course, risks must be assessed by well-qualified members of staff and an effective supervision process put in place. Parents and families should be informed of this process and of the setting's recognition that children cannot learn without some risk and that those children who are exposed to no risk at all are more likely to suffer accidents as they have built up no coping strategies. That said, it cannot be too strongly stated that every time the outside area is set up, equipment such as the climbing frame should be checked for stability, locks on gates should be checked for security, the sand pit for cleanliness and the wheeled toys for wobbly wheels! Children are entitled to an environment that is safe for them to experiment in and any risk must be manageable and professionally assessed.

The outside area provides the possibilities for an inclusive environment in ways that are sometimes harder to produce indoors. For children who find cognitive learning hard, may well excel in their physical development. The child with, for example, a severe hearing loss can run fast, climb, ride bikes, plant seeds and tend the animals. The disability often hampers a child less in the outdoor learning environment where there is such a wide range of things at which they can succeed and be seen to be succeeding. It is in the garden that the shy child can gain comfort from stroking the guinea pigs. It is in the garden that friendships are often struck up between groups of children cooperatively constructing an obstacle course and it is in the garden where a very young child can gain the first delight that gardeners experience when their sunflower seed first sprouts and spends the summer growing taller than every member of the family!

Positive dispositions

The fact that the outdoor area is one of *provisions* rather than *activities* makes for a place where children often have more autonomy over what they do than is the case indoors. Provision allows children to use the equipment that has been set out in ways of their choosing, reflecting the EYFS reminder about learning and development that we should 'provide experiences that help children to develop autonomy and a disposition to learn'.[78] Children who have been reading the story of 'The Enormous Crocodile' at group time may be highly motivated to construct an area that is the 'sea' next to a boat or some dry land where they are safe from crocodiles. They will try their very hardest to complete the obstacle course circuit without their feet touching the ground or hide effectively behind the shrubs or knock down all the skittles in one go, letting us know that they are learning just as effectively in the outdoor area as they would do indoors.

The opportunities for children to think creatively and imaginatively in the outdoor area are directly related to the skill of the practitioners in making the environment interesting. This is directly related to what has been made available for children to play with. The tent or small den will stimulate a wide range of games about camping, being inside and outside and having picnics. At one nursery, a favourite summer game was known as 'toast in the tent' where children made toast under adult supervision, chose what to spread on the toast and then took it to the tent to incorporate in a pretend picnic. The theme became so popular that the children grew cress to spread on their toast and developed an ever-increasing range of preferences for spreads – marmite, hummus and lemon curd becoming the most popular. In this child-initiated, but adult-supported activity, practitioners saw children develop positive dispositions to trying a wide range of tastes while in a less formal eating situation than was customary. Here, children felt under no pressure if they rejected a disliked taste and they tended to try tastes that were unfamiliar as they saw their friends enjoying them.

In the same way, practitioners in the nursery described above often observed children 'writing' with the water brushes on the hard surface. Here again, a positive disposition to a complex and daunting task can be nurtured as a child can try out writing which can be rubbed out or dry up in the sun while still not confident enough to put pencil to paper when in a more formal setting.

Belonging and boundaries

This aspect of children's development, incorporating as it does, children's behaviour, sometimes causes anxiety amongst practitioners who see their control becoming less clearly defined in the outside area. As was stated in Chapter 1, children's behaviour is always linked to how they are feeling. A very clear set of expectations of behaviour needs to be in place for children to feel safe to explore the outside area to the full. If children feel that they are likely to be run into by an out-of-control tricycle or that they will get sand in their eyes from sand being thrown, they will not venture happily outside. Children and staff need to understand that the expectations of courtesy and learning are the same for both the inside and outside areas and that children have a right to feel that they can pursue their own playful learning uninterrupted. When children feel secure, they are more likely to engage in deep-level learning, and creative thinking and to feel confident about trying a new challenge.

Challenging behaviour in the outside area can nearly always be traced to a management problem. Careful observations may reveal such things as insufficient equipment, unclear expectations from staff as to how equipment is to be used or perhaps frustration at a lack of time or space for children to reach satisfactory conclusions to their projects.

For a child to truly feel that they belong to a setting, their cultural and linguistic heritage must be represented and valued. Dressing up provision, for example, must represent children's known experiences. For them to feel that they truly belong in a setting, the way that different lives are lived should be reflected out of doors as well as inside. So games played and natural resources available outside should be familiar to them.

The children's key person plays a central role in ensuring that all children feel confident in the outside area by being sensitively aware of what motivates them and what their anxieties might be. By observing and interacting appropriately, the key person can maximise the child's use of the outside by suggesting possibilities and supporting the child's own ideas. As the EYFS card reminds us 'The emotional environment is created by all the people in the setting, but adults have to ensure that it is warm and accepting of everyone'.[79]

So '**How should children feel about themselves and their learning in the outside area?'** The answer must be that they should feel confident to explore the range of opportunities that the garden has to offer, and in particular, those that are *only* available outside. They need to feel that their individual interests and their cultural practices are recognised and represented and that they have freedom to play with equipment flexibly so that they can exercise autonomy and begin to develop independence in their learning. Sensitive and responsive adults who observe and intervene as appropriate will be key in enabling children to feel truly at home in the setting's garden.

Children's cognitive and intellectual development

In this section the possibilities of learning new knowledge outside will be examined, as well as other aspects of children's cognitive development such as the encouragement of creativity, attitudes to learning and the role of the adult in observing and assessing children's learning.

Learning new knowledge

It might be wise, at the outset, to challenge the myth that the outside is not rich in intellectual learning opportunities. A glance at the picnic set and the outdoor dolls shows evidence of ample opportunities for children to count, to explore one-to-one correspondence, to match clothes to dolls and to plan menus and outings for the dolls.

Children playing with these dolls will be learning new mathematical concepts and practising already established ones as well as engaging their imaginative skills in devising a
picnic or a journey.

The sand and water play will, similarly, give children first-hand experiences of mathematical concepts. Often, useful restrictions are placed on the numbers of children playing with the sand and water; this limits numbers to ensure a higher quality of play. Thus,
children will begin to count to see whether there is room for them to play and then match
the numbers of buckets to the number of children to ensure that they have all that they
need. They will check the size of the buckets and notice that the larger ones hold more
sand or water and begin to match mathematical language to their play. This area of the
curriculum is one in which language plays a huge part and the children who have had a
lot of time playing with sand and water are those who will move more happily into learning concepts such as volume, capacity and the direction of water flow, with their associated language, as they progress through the Foundation Stage and later key stages.

Knowledge and understanding of the world is an area of the curriculum which is
well served by the outside. The concept of change is most successfully tackled here, as
children watch flowers develop from buds to seed heads and seasons change from hot
summer's sun to winter's frost and snow. Shadows pose intriguing questions for children
as they begin to ponder both the scientific and imaginative possibilities of shadows. In
'Everything Has a Shadow Except Ants',[80] children consider such questions as whether
their feet act as magnets, holding shadows in place and wondering if a bird's shadow
flies away with the bird. Such questions are a clear indication of children's cognitive
processes working at full speed as they try to make sense of experiences that skilful practitioners have made available to them. This is an excellent example of the mind going
through the sequence of adaption, assimilation and accommodation that Piaget considered in his research on young children's thought processes. In one early years setting,
practitioners placed a large mirror on a table in the garden and taped a roll of paper onto
the table next to it. Children looked into the mirror and watched the clouds floating
overhead. Some talked about what they could see while some drew the shapes that
appeared in the sky above. These first-hand experiences are the sort that give rise to children's questions about the world around them and act as a stimulus for staff to take learning to the next stage. The outside is a place where the skill of observation can be successfully taught; there is just so much that is interesting to note and so many changes since
the last time anyone looked, that 'noticing' can naturally become a habit of mind.

It is also outside that large-scale building projects can take place with their associated learning aspects. A group of children are digging a channel in the sand which they
want to run from one end to the other of the large sand pit so that they can make small
paper boats float the length of their newly constructed river. When the digging is complete they ask if it can be preserved and an adult helps them to write a sign that says
'Please leave'. The sign is then attached to a stick, which is implanted at the start point of
the digging. Thus, they have engaged with several areas of the curriculum simultaneously: knowledge and understanding of the world as they construct their trench; com
munication, language and literacy as they talk together and write their sign; and

personal, social and emotional as they negotiate turn taking. A rich, holistic learning experience indeed, yet just an everyday occurrence in a good setting.

Creativity and thinking skills

In Chapter 7 a definition of creativity is suggested. It is described as 'a process of seeing new possibilities'[81] and is at its most powerful when the 'knowing' and the 'feeling' aspects of a child's disposition are working together.

In a setting situated in a village location, children had been talking to practitioners about the night sky as darkness began to fall earlier in the autumn. In the outside area some children had been trying to make a den under some shrubs and then to make it even darker by pulling a blanket over the top to see if some stars might appear. In conversation with a practitioner it became clear that although they had associated darkness with stars, they had not understood that stars could only be seen in the sky and not in the 'roof' of their den. Confusion had partly been caused by several children asserting that they had stars on their bedroom ceilings at home. The practitioner asked some open-ended questions about the differences between 'inside' and 'outside' and a general discussion followed about the moon and the sun and where they could be found. Later, in a small-group time she read 'Can't You Sleep, Little Bear'[82] to build on the children's growing interest in the idea of night-time. Torches were added to the den and, following group-time discussions about the shapes made by groups of stars, one child brought a star map from home. Practitioners sorted both fiction and non-fiction books about the night sky to share with interested children and a theme developed which included the making of owls and bats in the workshop area. Children were able to take the original idea in different directions: some children, who were fascinated by stars, preferred to draw shapes such as the Great Bear, while other children asked for slippers and hot water bottles to take in the den and played imaginary games of overnight camping. In this way, many children's initiatives were followed and, yet, because their motivation remained high, staff were able to observe and assess significant learning taking place. Here the 'process of seeing new possibilities'[83] is seen in action as children apply all their powers of concentration to thinking creatively and make new connections in their knowledge. The knowledge that these children already had about the night – stars, bed clothes, routines and so on – provided the inspiration for deep and complex thinking.

In the outside sand pit of the nursery described above, some children wanted to construct a pulley system, having just read the story of 'The Lighthouse Keeper's Lunch'.[84] This proved problematic and much experimentation took place before the children involved sought the help of a nearby adult. Even then it was several sessions later (including a trip to a local hardware store) that a passable system was eventually constructed that worked sufficiently well for the children to be able to send their small basket of sandwiches down the line to be attacked by the hungry (paper) seagulls! Staff were surprised at how consistently the children struggled to make the pulley work despite all the inherent difficulties and were reminded that young children would concentrate and persist and solve the problem if the motivation is there. They were also interested to note that the children demanded real sandwiches and a pulley system that was accurate and effective. The boundaries between make believe and science were very clear! It is this sort of playful learning experience that helps children to develop skills and attitudes such as concentration, problem-solving, patience, self-confidence and enthusiasm that were outlined in Chapter 2.

So to the practitioner's question: '**How do I know where children are in their learning and how can I move them on?'**

The EYFS document states that to plan effectively practitioners should 'Start with the child'.[85] To know at what level children are operating means that the practitioner needs a good idea of what they know, understand, feel and can do. '*Where children are*' does not simply refer to their intellectual knowledge, but refers to all other areas of their development as well. How children feel about, for example, getting their hands dirty on a cold, rainy morning, may significantly affect their ability to use the digging equipment and thus their ability to develop gross motor skills or to learn about plants. Careful, ongoing, observations of individual children's learning needs provide evidence with which the next learning can be planned with confidence. The value of observations lies in its ability to provide *evidence* rather than *supposition*. It may be tempting to assume that we know our children well. and that, as observation is demanding on staff time, time spent on observation would be more usefully spent directly interacting with the children. However, it is much more likely that interventions by staff will be more appropriate and successful if some professional observations have been made and shared first. Sometimes observations confirm what we already thought about a child, but, more often than one might suppose, a very different picture emerges following objective and consistent note being taken of what is actually happening. Observations need to be shared with other staff members and to be used as a basis for planning. If, for example, it is noted that some children are reluctant to go outside, gentle enquiry and encouragement can be offered to support these reluctant outdoor explorers. If, however, observations are stored away in filing cabinets, they become useless. The only reason to watch children is to provide for their future learning by using the evidence gathered. This is often called formative assessment or assessment for learning. As a guide, it may be helpful to consider sharing *positive* observations with families – '*I've seen Joey write all the letters of his name for the first time today*' – but to incorporate *negative* observations – '*Julie is still struggling with naming primary colours*' – into the planning, providing interesting opportunities for her to practice naming colours and to provide adult support to help her succeed.

The outside offers rich opportunities to watch, listen and note as children are sometimes less constrained in the ways that they show what they know. A child who is intrigued by the tyre marks her bike has made when riding through a patch of water lying on the hard surface may be encouraged to take a print of it or to find other patterns that occur outside such as those on bark or the regular shapes of petals on sunflowers. The early learning goal for exploring and investigating supports just this approach by exhorting children to 'Look closely at similarities, differences, patterns and change'.[86] Looking closely, or noticing, is one of the key attributes of a successful learner and is an invaluable tool for lifelong learning.

The skill of the practitioner in knowing where children are and moving them on stems from the fundamental understanding that all we really know about children comes through what they show us and what they communicate to us. It behoves us, then, to get into good habits of listening to them, noting what they tell or show us and reflecting on how this knowledge can be used to further their development. The phrase 'active listening' effectively describes the attitude of practitioners that value what a child trying to communicate and responds sensitively to the message that is being conveyed.

Physical and motor development

The link has regularly been made between children's physical abilities and their later success with small motor skills such as writing and drawing. Indeed, Sally Goddard Blyth's work with older children suffering from dyslexia and attention deficit disorder seems to point to a relationship between the lack of regular physical play experiences that young children may have and their struggle with various dimensions of formal 'school work' later.[87]

Organisation and management

Children's physical and motor development is most successfully developed outdoors as they practice their gross motor skills by running, skipping, hopping, jumping, throwing and climbing. Even very young children benefit from being outside as they are learning stability in standing up and walking. Here there is space to push along the box of bricks on wheels and climb up grassy banks, perhaps covered with an old carpet, to enable them to experiment with uneven surfaces and small hillocks. For those children who spend a lot of their time in a pushchair, the outside area of the setting may be vital in providing the range of movement experiences that are needed for full healthy growth and physical development. For children to feel confident about playing with messy activities, there needs to be clear guidance about getting wet, muddy and sandy, especially if their parents have told them 'not to get dirty'. Parents may need to be helped to understand that Foundation Stage learning is essentially about trying things out, experimenting and practising. These processes are not, and cannot be, tidy and this is especially true of the outside area. Often settings will provide spare outdoor clothes or parents may like to provide their own, which can be worn for the most messy of activities. Only if parents truly understand the value of playful learning, of children experimenting, exploring and learning through first-hand experiences, will they appreciate the necessity of clothing their children appropriately. After all, when gardening, painting or decorating, we, as adults, wear our old clothes. Children need to do the same.

The organisation of the outside area needs as much careful planning as the curriculum content. Sometimes, the unaccustomed amount of space can confuse children, used as they are to operating in much smaller spaces. Smaller living areas have given rise to an unfamiliarity with the concepts of being able to 'spread out', and sometimes physical boundaries can help children organise their games and play so that conflicts with others are avoided. Climbing and jumping from a tree trunk or climbing frame needs extra physical space in the 'landing' area as children try to jump further and from a greater height. Children riding bikes or pushing prams through the landing areas may suffer if this expanding boundary is not monitored and adjusted! Physical boundaries can, and should, be negotiated with the children and a practitioner asking 'How much space do you think you will need for landing'? is very valuable in helping children to predict and develop spatial awareness as well as reminding them that the well-being of other children is paramount.

Helen Bilton recommends that the outside has specific 'learning bays' where each area has its own dimension or focus.[88] Certainly children need to be able to experience a range of provision and activities and different types of spaces so that they can be:

- messy
- hidden
- cooperative
- communicative
- noisy.

All these elements are as valuable as the tidier and quieter aspects of play and are more naturally catered for outside. Consultation with children is often effective when planning the outside area, as it is of huge importance to them and they will have no shortage of ideas and requests! They can be asked which areas they like best and why, as well as how to solve problems that may arise. Children can take photos of the part of the garden they like best, which can then be displayed in the setting alongside children's comments scribed by staff. This process helps to raise the status of the outside, both within and beyond the setting, as children, parents and visitors recognise that this is a valued and valuable part of the provision.

Outside for the very young

For the very young, the outside can also be a place of intrigue and delight. There need to be opportunities for reaching and grasping, for rolling and toddling, pushing and pulling, lying and rocking. There need to be protected areas where these gentler activities can take place alongside the more exuberant play of the older child. There should be places that are soft and comfortable such as rugs, grass, hammocks and laps. Treasure baskets with interesting things to grab, taste, listen to and feel can reflect the outside environment by concentrating on natural materials and there need to be shady places and small places for babies and toddlers to feel enclosed and safe.

Schematic play

Access to the outside is key to the young child's developing play patterns or schemas that we considered in Chapter 3. It is outside that there is enough room to practice running round and round when learning about circles or throwing a ball into the basketball net when learning what a trajectory action feels like. Two boys in the nursery described above were interested in the enveloping schema and began weaving a huge spider's web around the climbing frame with string. After a long morning's work, the climbing frame was certainly looking like a spider's web and much sensitive negotiation was needed for other children to appreciate the project and find other equipment to climb on for a day or so. The boys needed their work to be valued for a little while after it was finished and were helped to make a sign in the writing area that stated 'Please Leave'. Interestingly, even though the writing was an approximation of the words 'Please Leave' and not many of the children could read the sign, it became clear to all the children that a piece of paper with writing on and sellotaped to a construction meant that it was to be left alone. No child ever challenged this process and it became commonplace for children to save their creations for their parents or friends to admire before agreeing to them being dismantled.

'How can I ensure that resources are available for children to use actively and independently?'

A rich outdoor area will make the best use of the resources available, recognising that the word 'resources' applies not only to equipment such as the climbing frame and the gardening tools but also to *time*, *space* and *people*. These are some of the most valuable resources that a practitioner has and, when used wisely, can make all the difference to the child's learning experience in the outside. For example, if time spent in the outside area is brief, it is likely that it will be frantic, with children desperately anxious to be outside as soon as the door is open. They will then rush through the things they want to do as they know that all too soon they will have to return indoors. This does not provide a climate in which children can develop all those skills that were considered in Chapter 2 that are so valuable in deep-level learning such as concentration, persistence, problem-solving and patience. As much time as possible needs to be allocated to being outside and the door should be opened quietly so that children learn to move calmly between the inside and the outside. As Helen Bilton comments in her book 'Outdoor Play in the Early Years': 'Children can go from being builders outside, moving inside to make and write signs, moving back outside again to set up the signs.'[89] In practice, those settings which have allocated both as much time as possible to being outside and as much space as possible for large-scale activities, will find that children are learning at a much deeper level than those who find that they can only snatch brief opportunities to learn outside.

People are probably the most valuable resource that a setting has and are there to extend children's understanding. Sometimes this will be done by joining in with conversations, or perhaps by adding equipment that children ask for or offering suggestions that help children achieve their objectives. Staff will also help children join in with group play, thus contributing to a shy child's self-confidence, or intervene when unacceptable behaviour is happening. Recent research found that well-trained and knowledgeable staff raised children's ability to learn more than any amount of good-quality equipment.[90] For children to feel that they can use the outdoor equipment independently there needs to be a clear understanding amongst both staff and children that it is the children who

'As much space as possible for large-scale activities'

will usually decide how and where equipment will be played with in the garden. If they need some play people to put in the large sand area, that should be acceptable, though, of course, woodwork tools need to be under adult supervision and used only at the woodwork bench at all times. Even very young children soon become aware of the expectations or boundaries that are in place in their nursery when these boundaries are gently but consistently enforced. The result is an outside space where children feel that they are safe to follow their ideas without harm coming to them and free to play creatively and independently. Children under the age of six tend to be very effective self-managers of their learning, and the outside provides a rich environment to learn about exciting and wondrous things!

Social and language development

The outside area of the early years setting provides both challenges and unique opportunities for social interactions to take place. As the garden area often feels less structured than the inside, rules and boundaries are sometimes less clear to children who may have little experience of being outside. Ways of interacting thoughtfully towards each other, which come easily inside, are sometimes harder to remember in the excitement of a chasing game or the potential thrill of throwing the contents of a bucket of sand across the sand pit! Staff need to be very clear that the same boundaries of expectations are present both inside and outside. They need to consider as a staff what balance is to be kept between the freedoms that children have outside to be independent and the controls that are necessary for staff to maintain, which will, in effect, protect children's freedoms. An unsafe, chaotic and poorly resourced outside area can become a dangerous place as children struggle to play in an overcrowded space with resources that are unfit for purpose and with friends who are overexcited and therefore inconsiderate.

Conversely, the garden, when well provisioned, gives rise to 'enhanced social relations'.[91] It is in the garden that genuine conversations are easily maintained about such things as how many flies can be seen on a spider's web or whose is the tallest sunflower. The construction of an obstacle course by children requires not only a sophisticated use of language as problems are thought through but also negotiation as a child understands that her idea must give way to someone else's which has more chance of succeeding. It is hard to overstate the importance of this type of process in developing the young child's view of themselves in their immediate world of friends as they begin to learn about their rights and responsibilities within the community of their setting. Parents, when asked what they hope their children will learn from attending an early years setting, will often answer 'To mix well and make friends'. In my nurseries I was often surprised at this response, as I assumed that it was their children's intellectual development that concerned parents most. However, the majority of parents recognised that success in life depends rather more on being able to get along with others than it does on having a very high IQ. In Chapter 1, when the emotional and behavioural aspects of learning were considered, reference was made to the Startright Report, where it was stated that 'No-one learns successfully without motivation, social skills and confidence'.[92] It is in the outside area that these attitudes to learning are often seen being put to the test as children explore the nature of their relationships with each other.

While playing in the garden, children can *explore their rights and duties and practice the skills necessary for good citizenship* and *develop habits of mind which secure social changes without introducing disorder*. Of course, it is not only in the outside area that these types of learning experiences take place; however, they tend to happen more readily outside, where, because of the greater space available, the adults may be further away and there are opportunities for projects and negotiations to meander and progress in a more unstructured way.

Relationships with the environment

It is in the garden that young children are most likely to encounter plants, small animals and insects for the first time. For those living in inner city areas, the setting's garden may provide the only place where they can interact regularly with nature in this way.

For children with little experience of interacting with animals and insects, the nature of their interactions with small living things sometimes presents challenges. Staff may need to be vigilant as children take the heads off flowers to see more closely what is inside. Often, very young children have not developed a clear understanding of the differences between 'living and not living' and when encountering spiders, ants, worms and ladybirds can be rather heavy handed! Sometimes practitioners find this upsetting but should recognise that, as in all areas of learning, it is the lack of experience that leads to inappropriate behaviour and a consistent gentle approach by staff is usually all that is needed to instil a culture of 'watch but do not harm' when it comes to small living things. Children are capable of developing great interest in growing plants and vegetables that may remain with them all their lives. These early interactions with wildlife similarly provide starting points for a respect for and a desire to protect the natural world, which this generation of children will need to harness if the fight against climate change is to be won. Recent research has substantiated these ideas. Vaealiki and Mackey describe how they found in their 2008 research that 'caring can ripple out from children's engagement with the outdoor environment towards their relationships with peers, their teachers and their families'.[93] Certainly, a sustainable future is more likely to be achieved if we can expose children to non-human inhabitants of our planet and teach them attitudes of care and respect towards them.

Learning new language

Language in the outside area often flourishes as children's curiosity is aroused by new and different experiences. Conversation flows as they describe the appearance of frog-spawn in the old sink at the end of the garden or notice how yesterday's tight green poppy bud is today, a huge blowsy red flower. New scientific vocabulary is necessary here as they learn the difference between a 'snail' and a 'caterpillar'. Concepts that are unique to the outside such as wind and rain provide opportunities to widen vocabulary as they experience 'splashing' and 'gusts'. Descriptions are also prompted by what can be seen outside. A 3-year-old child will talk about the leaves 'dancing' in the autumn or a butterfly 'flitting' from flower to flower. To embed and reinforce this 'outdoor' language it is helpful to follow up outdoor experiences with stories or general knowledge books which can take children's interest further.

Because social development and language development are intrinsically linked, the practitioner's question for this area of development is '**How should we all act towards each other?'**
The role of the adult is crucial in setting the tone of behaviour in the outside area. Practitioners will find that much time is spent working with children on how to get the equipment and space that they need to complete their game or project in an acceptable way. Children may have been used to taking what they need and will have to be supported as they learn that words are effective too! Simple phrases such as *'Please may I have that'*? and *'I haven't finished with it yet'* will transform the feel of the setting to one where pushing and snatching are seen by children to be unnecessary as negotiations replace them. This work, although costly in terms of time, will reap huge benefits as children become more calm and can concentrate their efforts on their investigations free from unwelcome interruptions. There is, of course, a related resourcing issue here. If children are expected to plant runner beans and look for ladybirds with a degree of

independence, there must be enough trowels and magnifying glasses to go round for children to be able to negotiate sharing them.

Adults will need to be on hand in the garden to:

- plan and set up the play provision and to adapt it flexibly as situations change during the session
- challenge unacceptable attitudes that threaten inclusive practices
- observe children before interacting with their play
- inform records of achievement and thus inform planning
- supervise to ensure a safe environment
- mediate and to support children who find aspects of outdoor play difficult.

Staff will also find that how they behave to each other will be reflected by how the children behave towards each other. Adults who are respectful of each other, who are careful of the non-human inhabitants of the garden and who convey a genuine delight at the wonders to be discovered outside will find that children will be able to access more confidently all that the garden has to offer.

Books and stories

Give daily opportunities to share and enjoy a wide range of fiction and non-fiction books.[94]

As we are focusing on areas of the setting which children use rather than areas of the curriculum, in this chapter the decision has been made to concentrate on particular aspects of literacy. The aspects are children's literacy development that will be considered in this chapter are speaking, listening, reading and authorship. It is these skills that are most usually based in and around the book corner, although, as we shall see, there are opportunities to meet up with one's favourite stories and to think up new ones in many different areas of a well-run setting. Other aspects of literacy such as writing will not be ignored but explored in depth in Chapter 9.

The successful book area is one which offers a wide range of learning experiences to the young child. It is not solely concerned with developing communication, literacy and language skills, although, of course, it will do just that.

A warm, comforting and rich book area will provide emotional security, and opportunities to be together and companionable as well as being a place to learn new knowledge. It draws on the familiar and much loved feelings which stem from being cuddled by a parent or carer at home as well as providing stories about experiences that are new and challenging. It is vitally important that this area is carefully thought about and planned so that its maximum potential is realised. Here is how it might look.

The book area

The book area in this rural early years setting is situated not far from the main entrance but not so near that draughts are drawn in on chilly winter mornings! It is tucked round a corner from where the children's coats and wellie boots are stored so that it becomes a natural 'next port of call' for parents and children once they have hung up their coats at the start of the session. Both time and space are built in for a few adults and children to sit on an old sofa and look at some books or just talk together quietly.

The area is not newly furnished: in fact, the sofa is over 20 years old but it is big and comfortable and has a bright 'throw' and some comfortable cushions. On the floor is some carpet, again not new, but clean and donated by a parent who did not need it any more. Onto this carpet, staff have placed some big floor cushions and a low table on which they spread some books that fitted in with their topic and that some of the children have especially liked and wanted to share with their families.

Books are arranged on white-covered shelving that almost surrounds the carpet so that there is an enclosed feel to the area. All the books can be reached by the children and they are tidied each session so that they look well cared for and not torn when the children arrive. There is an interesting mix of books. Staff have taken into account the fact that there are more boys in the setting than girls, and that boys sometimes find books less enthralling than girls do. Therefore they have incorporated a substantial number of non-fiction books about machinery, dinosaurs and some well-known superheroes in order to encourage the boys to take an interest in books. There are big books, but also miniature books which the children love as well as the usual range of paperback books and some of the books that children have made themselves. There are books about children from different cultures and stories about children who experience very different lives from those who attend the setting.

There is a library system in place where children can borrow books to take home. This is so popular that staff have had to introduce a 'reference only system' at times to enable them to keep some books that they need for teaching purposes in the setting! Some books go home and are lost under beds, which worries some practitioners, but the manager has decided that it is better that books are keenly borrowed and read, occasionally lost and then replaced than that they stay on the shelves in the setting.

During each session, children are able to access the area whenever they want unless they are taking part in a small-group activity. A practitioner, a visitor or a family member is often to be found reading to a small number of children during the day.

This book area sends out several messages by how it is furnished and used. One of these is that the setting welcomes families to use it and facilitates this by not requiring children to rush past it to a group registration at the beginning of the session. Children in this setting go to whichever part of the provision they choose on arrival and, although the book area is a favourite, it is a permanent fixture so that children know they can return to it regularly.

Another message that this area sends out is that it functions as a link between the setting and the world outside. Most of the books on the shelves are those that the children have seen either at home or in the library or on the TV and so there is a comforting reminder of sitting, cuddled with parents, grandparents or carers in an emotionally secure environment. A further message is that this is a place where adventures can happen. Books tell stories of magical events, sometimes scary and sometimes challenging, but which are resolved in the companionship of a trusted adult. They take children to different worlds and teach new ideas and knowledge. To draw children into all these possibilities, the area must be inviting, cosy, unhurried and permanent. It must be a valued part of the provision by all who use it.

In Chapters 1–4 we considered the theory underpinning children's emotional, physical, social and cognitive development. In this chapter we will take those aspects of

'Books take children to different worlds'

development in turn and think about how they can be catered for in the book area of the setting. As usual, we will also consider the associated practitioner questions.

We need, at this point, to consider very carefully which books we feel are good enough to place in the book corner, because this is crucial in furthering a deep level of learning and a sound progression. Before any book is added to the setting's collection it must be subjected to the following fundamental question, *'Is this a good book?'* To answer this question, practitioners must consider the following aspects of a book:

- Its *appearance*. Does it look attractive, though not necessarily brightly coloured. Is it hard wearing and can children handle it easily?
- The *storyline*. If it interests the adults, then it will probably interest the children.
- The *illustrations*. Children should be offered pictures that are in other formats than cartoons.
- The *story*. Does this book have something worthwhile to say? This does not have to be necessarily a didactic message, but it must be worth the time that has been spent reading it!
- The *hidden agenda*. Often, books are suggesting attitudes, ideas and new ways of thinking that may give children either the permission to feel in a certain way, or help creative thinking.
- The *text*. Does the way the print looks on the page help children to follow the story by giving clues as to meaning?

If your answer to the majority of these questions is *'yes'*, then the book in question is probably worth its place on your bookshelf. If the answer is *'no'*, be ruthless because there are plenty of wonderful books, written by children's authors and not put together by literary teams, which will further children's development cognitively, socially and emotionally.

Emotional and behavioural development

Provide stories, pictures and puppets which allow children to experience and talk about how characters feel.[95]

Self-esteem

Children feel deep emotions which are not always easily expressed, particularly when their language skills are still developing. Good books contain many different emotions in their pages: laughter, fear and empathy, to name but a few. They deal in depth with emotional human events such as friendships, being different and being in pain. Children can identify with stories, recognise their emotions within the pages and feel confident that their emotions are recognised and accepted. This recognition raises children's self-esteem and in turn helps them to deal with what are, sometimes, difficult emotions.

The following are just a few emotions and social events in children's lives which are considered in children's books (you will be able to find many more):

A Dark, Dark Tale by Ruth Brown[96]
The Tunnel by Anthony Browne[97]
Although both these books deal with the fundamental feelings of fear, they are resolved in very different ways.

Once There Were Giants by Martin Waddell[98]
Grandpa and Thomas by Pamela Allen[99]
These book consider loving family relationships that offer consistency in changing times.

Some Dogs Do by Jez Alborough[100]
This book considers the emotions involved in being different

Lost and Found by Oliver Jeffers[101]
This book illustrates the strength of friendship and the deep sadness that the absence of the friend can cause.

There's No Such Thing As a Dragon by Jack Kent[102]
The Magic Bed by John Burningham[103]
These two books tackle the intriguing possibility that grown-ups are sometimes wrong. This possibility is challenging for young children who do not naturally

think that this is a possibility. They usually find this aspect of these books captivating, as it is an idea that opens up new ways of thinking!

The Paper Bag Princess by Robert Munsch[104]
The Three Little Wolves and the Big Bad Pig by Eugene Trivizas and Helen Oxenbury[105]
These books are for older children, and are two of many children's books that consider well-known tales but with a twist. These two stories both have a moral component as they question common assumptions: one challenges the qualities associated with being a princess; the other, the guilt of the wolf. These books, and others like them, help children to feel in different ways and enable them to accept that others may feel and think differently from them.

Brown Bread and Honey by Pamela Allen[106]
This book tackles the topical issue of lack of exercise and obesity.

Where the Wild Things Are by Maurice Sendak[107]
This book looks at how a child might feel when he has been "naughty" and what the consequences might be.

On The Way Home by Jill Murphy[108]
This book is always a favourite as it is so easy for a child to identify with Claire, the heroine's, need to be brave by inventing tales of derring-do until finally collapsing in tears as she reaches home.

Positive dispositions

Well-chosen books are central to practitioners' strategy to develop a positive disposition towards reading. There is no more powerful tool than delight in a good story to encourage children to pick up books and show an interest in the business of decoding the print in order to find out what happens between the pages. To 'provide experiences that help children to autonomy and a disposition to learn',[109] the book area must, as we have seen, be accessible, attractive and full of interesting books so that children and adults are genuinely drawn to its contents. Planning for the area needs to ensure that there are adults available to read stories to children as well as having books which contain mainly pictures so that children can access their meaning by themselves or together with their friends. To encourage successful use of this area and thereby preserving a positive disposition to reading, it may be worth considering suggesting that some books are best for 'being read to by an adult' and some are for 'reading by myself'. However, many books that adults usually read to children can be enjoyed by children without an adult present as they retell a well-loved story and describe to themselves and to their friends what is happening in the pictures.

Another way to encourage a positive disposition to reading is to help children make up their own stories, often based on well-known tales, and make these stories into books that sit on the shelves alongside commercially produced ones. Homemade versions of stories such as *The Enormous Turnip,* with real children substituted for the old man, his wife, the dog, the cat and the mouse, are hugely popular and can be acted out as well as read. Variations of *On The Way Home* by Jill Murphy,[110] and *Mr Gumpy's Outing*[111] by John Burningham work well in this format too.

Using stories as a basis for an interactive display provides an incentive for children to play and read at the same time. The *Bears In the Night*, by Jan and Stan Berenstain[112] has a simple text that is easily sectioned into short phrases that can be mounted onto pieces of card and placed alongside the relevant section of the display. Thus, children will eagerly tell each other *'that card says "Up Spook Hill"'* and place the appropriate phrase near the model of the scary hill upon which sits the owl whilst attaching *'through the rocks', 'down the tree'* and *'Whooo!'* to the right part of the display. They are, of course, reading the labels, but, as it is a playful game, it does not feel nearly as intimidating a process as tackling the same phrases in the book.

The Gruffalo by Julia Donaldson[113] is another story that lends itself to being played with. Children will be eager to play the parts of the mouse, the fox, the owl, the snake and the Gruffalo and can remember the words easily as it is written in such an attractive rhyming format. The book will be needed as a reference to ensure that everyone has got the action in the right order, of course. This is where a helpful adult can draw children's attention to the text. This story alone has been responsible for encouraging a positive disposition to read in many young children, as the mix of emotions in the strong storyline draws skilfully on their inherent curiosity and desire to join in and find out what happens. Even when they know what happens, they will ask for the same story again and again as the sense of excitement mounts each time as the story progresses. The immense feeling of satisfaction at the end is repeated and they will gain an increased confidence in decoding print each time they open the book and find that they can make even more meaning from the pages.

Supporting children's positive dispositions to reading

In order to provide meaningful support to young children who are at the beginning of their attempts to grasp some really complex concepts about literacy, knowledgeable adults are the key factor in their confident progression. At Sheffield Hallam University, Peter Hannon and Cathy Nutbrown (1997) developed a framework whereby adults could raise children's literary achievement by offering Opportunities, Recognising achievements, Interacting and Modelling behaviour and attitudes (ORIM).[114] Although designed for use by parents, it can be helpful when training practitioners because it is much about the attitudes of adults as it is about what they need to do. The (ORIM) framework,[115] is simple in design but has been proved to be effective possibly because it concentrates on giving children what they need developmentally to succeed in literacy and not just on a list of actions that need to be taken. ORIM covers the full range of literacy skills and is implemented across the whole range of children's activities. If, as suggested, adults offer opportunities for children to look at books and become familiar with stories, if adults recognise children's delight and achievements by interacting with responsiveness and enthusiasm and they read regularly with children, a culture of literacy will be developed within the setting. Put simply, if children's important adults show by their actions that books and stories are important to them, children will absorb this message and want to belong to the 'literary club'. In terms of teaching literacy to young children, this method of encouraging a positive disposition towards reading is far more powerful and effective than any number of sound sessions on the mat!

Belonging and boundaries

Enjoying books and stories is the vital component that children need to become competent readers. Although being able to decode print by phonological awareness plays a large part in the business of learning to read, it is by no means the most important part. There is no point in mastering the complex skills involved in decoding print if there is nothing you really want to read and this is the position that many young children find themselves in at school. So much attention is now given to the mechanics of reading that the excitement mentioned above – that of following a genuinely good story with its satisfactory resolution – is in danger of becoming lost. Along with this loss is the reluctance of the positive disposition to read that we considered in Chapter 1 and, as the desire to read fades, children are left with a lack of enthusiasm which can sink fast into disaffection and failure.

Readers can be thought of as belonging to a 'club' where they can be seen to have skills that unlock new worlds. These worlds are broadly of two kinds: one of usefulness and one of creativity. Margaret Meek states that 'It (reading) is useful not only for catching trains but also to tap into ways of knowing that have been accumulating over the centuries'.[116] Functional literacy – for example, being able to read timetables, newspapers and fill in forms – is the 'club' that enables people to manage their lives on a daily basis. It is this function of literacy that the government is most concerned with. The other type of 'club' is the one concerned with rhymes, tales and stories that reflect the culture in which we live, the creative business of authorship and the deep sense of belonging that comes from knowing traditional literature. Children who know that they belong to this club are those who are familiar with nursery rhymes and fairy stories and who, at their early years setting, can say to themselves 'I know this one' when a practitioner begins to retell the story of 'Little Red Riding Hood' or 'Goldilocks and The Three Bears'. The comfort that this feeling of belonging gives to young children is immense and it is fundamental to their subsequent ability to enjoy the fun of stories that are variations on a well-known tales. Examples of these are 'Jim and the Beanstalk' by Raymond Briggs[117] and 'The Three Little Wolves and the Big, Bad Pig' by Eugene Trivizas.[118]

The feeling of belonging, then, is crucial to developing the self-confidence that is needed to tackle the mountainous task of learning to read. Practitioners need to ensure that the book area and group-time stories reflect those that are a part of all their children's lives at home and that they value the informal literacy that has been a part of children's lives from their very earliest days.

There are, of course, some 'boundaries' that need to be instilled with the provision of good-quality books. Some children will not be experienced enough to know that books need to be cared for, must not be drawn on, cut or crumpled, as this lessens the enjoyment for others. Children who have not owned many books or have not belonged to the local library are those who are most likely to need help with this code of conduct. Although distressing for some practitioners to see books mishandled, it is a part of learning at this stage of development, like every other aspect of the Foundation Stage, and children will need differing levels of help. The pride that will result from being able to turn pages and follow a story sequentially through a book from the start to the finish and to begin to pick out some letters and words in the print is well worth the time and staff input necessary. Working with children at this level is really valuable in helping them to join the 'literacy club' and to begin to see the riches that books have to offer. In other words, those children who have come to love stories such as 'The Gruffalo' are more likely to take care of the books between whose pages the excitement of the story lies!

So, **How should children feel about themselves and their learning?**
In the book area, the prevailing feelings of children as they approach the comforting cushions and sofa should be those of confidence, belonging and curiosity. They will wish to see the story they enjoyed yesterday and check that it is just as satisfying today. They will feel confident enough to be drawn into a new story, especially if the author is one they already know. They will feel that they belong to this area if they see their lives and their culture represented in the books around them and they will feel they can rise to the challenge of making meaning from the pages if there are interested adults on hand to share in the task.

Children's cognitive and intellectual development

In this section the possibilities of learning new knowledge from books and stories will be examined, as well as other aspects of children's cognitive development such as the encouragement of creativity, attitudes to learning and the role of the adult in observing and assessing children's learning.

Learning new knowledge

Since time immemorial, books have provided the basis of new knowledge. They have been potent symbols of freedom of thought and have been instruments of power. Because understanding their contents opens up so many opportunities, learning to read is always thought of as a key indicator of successful learning. Currently, however, as we have seen above, the mechanics of meaning-making has triumphed over the desire to learn new knowledge from books, with children's disposition to read waning with each new set of statistics. New knowledge now comes from a wider range of sources, with the internet providing ever-updated information from a vast network of contributors. In whatever form new information is offered, it still needs to be interpreted, considered and commentated on, so that the reader is not a passive but active participant in the process.

It was the Cox Report[119] that stressed that the reader is an *active* participant, thus recognising Piaget's view that children construct their own meaning as they explore their world. In the world of literacy, each child needs to construct meaning from the pages of a book for themselves; it is not a process that can be 'done to' them. Perhaps it would be useful at this point to think how we might define a reader.

There are, as we have seen, two major components to reading: one aspect can be thought of as *interest and motivation* and the other can be thought of as *knowledge and expertise*.

In the *interest and motivation*, component, the reader:

- chooses to read and understands that reading is worthwhile
- sometimes wants to share and discuss what has been read
- actively responds to what has been read
- loves books and readily turns to a book.

However, in the *knowledge and expertise* component, the reader:

- deciphers print for a purpose
- expresses ideas and opinions about what they are reading

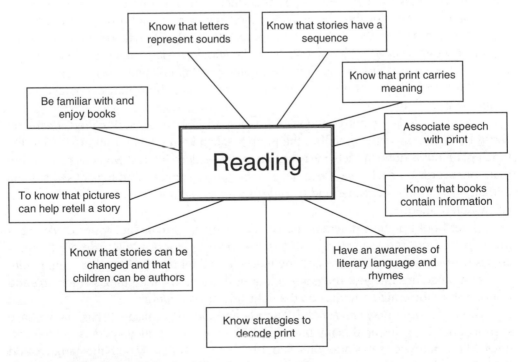

'Early knowledge about reading'

- understands that print carries meaning
- can construct meaning from print in the environment
- has a range of strategies to make meaning from print
- understands how stories work
- can identify with what is read and relate it to their own experience
- can predict possible outcomes
- brings prior experience to the text and can comment on the plot
- can select a book independently and with confidence
- can select a book by skimming and scanning the text
- understands that books can be shared
- has knowledge of how language works, such as rhyming, rhythms and alliteration.

New knowledge, as Jerome Bruner reminds us, can be given to anyone at any stage of development as long as it is honestly done and respects the level of understanding that the child has reached: see the discussion of the spiral curriculum in Chapter 2. There are many story books that do just this and through their compelling storyline give children access to what is sometimes complex new knowledge. Take for example, *Mr Archimedes' Bath* and *Alexander's Outing*, both by Pamela Allen,[120] which examine in a delightful story format the principles involved in buoyancy and displacement. These stories, like so much other rich literature such as John Bunyan's *Pilgrim's Progress* and Phillip Pullman's *His Dark Materials* work at different levels so that readers who are at an early stage of understanding can enjoy the story at face value. As they revisit a book with more maturity and understanding, they will begin to appreciate the scientific theories that are being explored within its pages. These two Pamela Allen books in particular provide wonderful opportunities for practitioners to link stories with practical experiments, or as the foreward of *Mr Archimedes' Bath* so aptly warns, 'This charming book may encourage messy experiments at bath time'![121]

New knowledge is not confined to science, of course. A book called '*Beans on Toast*' by Paul Dowling[122] describes the journey taken by the bean from the field to the lunch plate but is done in such a way as to grip the reader's interest while using no more than four words on each page! It contains information, humour and logical sequencing that appeal to the new reader and provides so many picture clues that the meaning is easily determined.

Other books provide different knowledge a similar format. The stories of *The Very Busy Spider* and *The Very Hungry Caterpillar*, both by Eric Carle,[123] explore the processes of spiders' weaving webs and the lifecycle of the butterfly. They draw the reader in with a range of strategies. There are colourful illustrations, intriguing sequencing and a strong storyline which stays just on the right side of non-fiction.

The Lighthouse Keeper's Lunch by Ronda and David Armitage[124] has, as we have seen in Chapter 5, inspired many practitioners to construct pulley systems in their settings. Mairi Hardwick sets stories on a Scottish island,[125] which by both the narrative and the beautiful watercolour illustrations, gives children who have no concept of islands a real taste of what life there might be like. These are just a few examples of rich books that will teach children new knowledge; practitioners will, of course, have many of their own favourites.

Decoding print

The section above concentrated on two aspects of reading: first, the kinds of new knowledge that children can learn from them; and, secondly, the many strategies that authors use to draw in the reader to take an active part in discovering meaning. Whereas authors place importance on the quality of the story and illustrations to encourage children into their books the National Literary Strategy requires that:

Beginning readers should be taught:

- grapheme–phoneme correspondences in a clearly defined, incremental sequence
- to apply the highly important skill of blending (synthesising) phonemes in the order in which they occur, all through a word to read it
- to apply the skills of segmenting words into their constituent phonemes to spell
- that blending and segmenting are reversible processes.

This is in somewhat stark contrast to much of the research that looks at how most children will acquire the ability to read. The body of research suggests that, rather than being able to build up sounds from their smallest components, children have a tendency to recognise whole words, or letters from those words. These are often those nouns that they learned to speak first and, in particular, their name. Research finds that less formal literary experiences in the home are clear predictors of later success in reading and place a significant emphasis on close, loving interactions and a rich oral language environment. For example, Ninio and Bruner (1983) found that 'book reading by mothers and their children aid the development of grammar, of communication and later literacy skills'[126] and that 'inference skills', which very young children develop in the home environment, can be built on by practitioners to very good effect. This latter research suggests that:

teachers should know and nurture the key characteristics of good inferencers. These are:

- being an active reader who wants to make sense of a text
- monitoring one's own comprehension and resolving misunderstanding as one is reading
- having a rich vocabulary
- having a good working memory.[127]

and that these are recognisable predispositions of a reader. They go on to suggest that the modelling of reading behaviour by practitioners will tend to develop these inferences in children not yet showing them. It seems sensible to suggest, therefore, that a 'broad brush' approach to the teaching of reading may offer more success than the mechanical option alone. In fact, as this chapter is being written, David Reedy, president of the UK Literacy Association, has stated that 'More attention needs to be paid to the other elements of what it means to be a reader as well as the phonics element. Phonics is necessary but it is not sufficient to become a reader in the rounded sense'.[128]

The Early Years Curriculum Group had already expressed grave anxieties in December 2006 by stating that 'it is wrong to expect a child not yet able to pronounce words clearly to be capable of decoding phonetically'. They go to suggest that 'teaching phonics too soon risks damaging children's sense of achievement and self worth' and that they 'can learn phonics very quickly later on when they are efficient communicators'. The Early Years Curriculum Group advocated concentrating on fostering a love of books and stories and developing early reading through children's play. This latter strategy, we will consider in the final chapter, which considers teaching the curriculum in a holistic way through a balance of adult-led and child-initiated projects.

Creativity and thinking skills: encouraging authorship

Good children's literature makes powerful links between the ways children think about things and possible new ways of thinking. EYFS Card 4.3 calls this 'transforming understanding' and the phrase aptly describes the process that we all go through when using our existing knowledge as a stepping stone from where we can move to a new place in our understanding. In the process of Piaget's 'assimilation, accommodation and adaptation', a book can gently pose an alternative viewpoint for the child to consider. Take, for example, the stories in the book *Time to Get out of the Bath, Shirley* by John Burningham.[129] In this book, the author skilfully weaves two stories together. The first story is a very tedious one of Shirley's mother's uninspiring comments as Shirley takes her bath. To escape from the boredom, Shirley lets her imagination take over and, by using the very clever devise of using no words but brightly coloured illustrations, the author takes us into the second story, of Shirley's escape down the plughole to a land of knights, castles and jousting on inflatable floating ducks! This second story asks children to use their creative thinking skills by suggesting that there are alternatives to the expected turn of events. The beauty of a book such as this is that a child may question their existing knowledge about changing size and decide that, in Piaget's terms, their current knowledge about the nature of baths and plugholes is correct and that it is not possible to slip down plugholes and play with kings and queens. Of course, the joy is that in books, as in their play, anything is possible.

The book *Rosie's Walk* by Pat Hutchins[130] offers similar opportunities for children to be creative with a story and to question the obvious plot. The joy, once again, is in the second plot which, with no words, gives children the chance to use their own words to describe both the disasters that befall the fox and how they might feel about his misfortunes.

Books such as this will help children *'transform their understandings'* by suggesting alternative ways of thinking about things and offering freedom from the straightjacket of 'right' or 'wrong' answers and the tedium of obvious solutions.

We considered in Chapter 2 the attitudes to learning that will help children towards creative and critical thinking. These were:

- concentration
- problem-solving
- patience
- self-confidence
- enthusiasm.

A good book that will 'nourish children's thinking', i.e. challenge their powers of lateral thinking and ask them to delve deeply into the book's meaning, will both require these attitudes and help children to develop them.

Critical thinking skills are key in the progress towards autonomy and independence. Going 'beyond the given meanings –and forge something new'[131] as we considered in Chapter 1, gives children agency and a real sense of self-worth and individuality and books such as those we have thought about in this chapter give children just those kinds of opportunities. If we take, for example, *On the Way Home* by Jill Murphy,[132] we can immediately find issues that can entice children to concentrate, solve problem and think laterally. Once the basic story of Claire's journey home with her already grazed knee has been established and the range of explanations to her friends have been considered, children can be invited to question whether Claire's version of events bears any relation to reality. They might ask:

- If not, why might she be inventing these preposterous stories?
- Is it ethical to make up a series of imagined events to her friends who show a genuine concern for her well-being?
- Might the reason be that she needs to concentrate on these tales to keep from crying?
- Can the reader be empathetic on the last page when she arrives home and at last, feels safe to cry?
- Can children make up a similar story using their own name and thinking up different disasters that happen along the way?

A questioning approach to literature such as this helps even very young readers to become active participants in the business of reading and impose their own ideas, beliefs and judgements on the text. This seemingly straightforward process introduces children to the freedom and controls of creativity, as defined in the introduction to *All Our Futures* (p 4,DfEE 2000). It states 'The creative process involves using imagination, pursuing purposes, being original and judging value'. It goes on to assert that 'Creative processes require both the freedom to experiment and the use of skills, knowledge and understanding'.[133] One can see, then, that within the freedom to experiment with the basic story of *On the Way Home*, and to make a successful story of their own, children need to understand how the story works. They need to have a knowledge of the sequencing of the events and an understanding of how the story is resolved on the last page.

They need to keep to the pattern of the repeating phrase 'And that's how I got my bad knee' and to be able to replicate the atmosphere of danger and impending disaster which occurs on every page!

These, then, are perhaps not such a simple set of requirements as may have been originally thought and a secure familiarity with the book is essential before a child can assume ownership of a variation of the text. However, when achieved, children will delight in their creative skills and search eagerly for another text which they can give the same treatment. Practitioners will soon become adept at discovering those which are the most adaptable to this processes and take pride in their children's growing abilities to think critically and creatively.

The practitioner's question associated with children's cognitive and intellectual development is this: '**How do I know where children are in their learning and how can I move them on?'.**

The reading section of the Early Years Profile document gives clear pointers to what stage a child has reached along the road to becoming a reader. Many of the accompanying scenarios by which a practitioner can decide on how far a child has progressed are helpful and accurate. They are useful in helping us assess at what point a child is in their learning but, on the whole, the Profile does not specify which adult *behaviours* will encourage a child to read.

Encouraging children to read is, of course, more than assessing where they are and it is more than teaching decoding exercises such as synthetic phonics. The most valuable asset that practitioners have in this task of developing literacy is their own genuine love of books and stories which they want to share with children. The confidence to tackle such a complex cognitive challenge as reading requires a high level of self-esteem and the reassurance of a loved and trusted adult. Words on the page are, as we know, symbolic representations of meanings. The young child has to be confident with the concept of symbolism – that one thing can stand for something else – and have been practising it for a very long time, as we saw in Chapter 2. Practitioners, with their in-depth knowledge of their key children's levels of development, are in exactly the right place to offer texts that are at an appropriate level to match the child's interests and abilities. This, together with offering many opportunities for children to talk, not only about the books they are becoming familiar with but also all the things that are important to them in their lives both inside and outside the setting, is a key feature of good practice, moving children towards literary competency.

To support children's authorship, practitioners should delight in children's made-up stories and offer to record them if this is what the children want. These recordings can then become homemade books which children want to return to again and again as they revel in the pride of having 'made a book'.

A helpful way to stimulate rich conversation in children who are not yet reading print is to share with them some of the many beautiful picture books that are available. These have no worrying words that may intimidate but do stimulate conversation about the stories contained in the pictures. These books are valuable both in giving children and adults interesting things to talk about and also giving very early readers access to books that they can relate to, encouraging the feeling that books are for them and that they, too, belong to the 'literacy club'.

Most importantly of all, practitioners need to allocate time to the book area! Children will be encouraged to go there if there are people available to share stories with them. If there is a shortage of staff, then parents, carers, students, grannies and visitors can all be utilised and, if the area has been attractively and comfortably arranged, these temporary storytellers may well not complain! Remember, also, that *telling* stories is just as valuable a process as reading them so if there are adults who prefer to tell stories or talk about their lives, this should be welcomed too. It all contributes to our rich literary heritage, helps the setting to feel grounded within its community and helps children to feel that adults are committed, one way or another, to literacy.

Social and language development

As we considered in Chapter 4, children's social development is intertwined with their language development. Nowhere is this more clearly evident than in the book area. Children's developing sense of self, their growing relationships with others and their relationship with their environment are all nurtured through the sensitively organised book area. The resourcing of this area of provision needs to reflect children who can identify with the pictures they see. There needs to be a careful balance of books that are about young children like them, about their parents, grandparents, brothers and sisters. There must be stories reflecting a range of family situations, single parents, step-parents and same-sex couples from different culture's so that children can both identify with what they read but also learn about families that are significantly different from theirs. *Staying at Sam's,* by Jenny Hessell[134] is an example of a book that explores the social dilemma of experiencing families that are different from one's own.

As children grow in their abilities to relate to others, so too will their skills in empathy. Their tolerance of their friends' differences will be treated with a newly developed sense of tolerance and sensitivity. This stage of social development also encompasses the idea that actions have consequences, and it at this point of developing empathy that adults can begin to reason with young children about what might be the result of a certain course of action. Many story books are based on experiences that children have when an action is seen to have consequences and these are helpful to a child wrestling with behavioural dilemmas. The consequences of actions, both individual and global, are dealt with both realistically and magically in the following stories:

> *Six Dinner Sid,* by Inga Moore[135]
> This story concerns the rather underhand and secretive behaviour of Sid, the cat, towards his dinner, which rebounds on him in due course. Children will discuss the dilemmas and their resolution enthusiastically with a range of ideas and the occasional hint of moral judgement!

Dogs Never Climb Trees, by Lynley Dodd[136]
This book deals with stereotyping and common misconceptions and how these can be challenged. In a very gentle way, Schnitzel Von Krumm, the dog with his 'very short legs and his very low tum' proves the reader wrong by his unexpected abilities that change ideas of what is possible.

Harry, The Dirty Dog, by Gene Zion[137]
In this dog story, the consequences of becoming unrecognisably grubby may be more fantastic than realistic, but the dilemma is real enough for Harry, the dog, and does address issues such as his behaviour causing the loneliness of rejection and the joy of once again belonging to the family that he had perhaps not appreciated enough.

Where the Wild Things Are by Maurice Sendak[138]
This book uses a similar format to explore how actions lead to what, at first, feels like a desirable, illicit, freedom but which, in the long term, cause isolation and a longing to be reunited.

Dear Zoo by Rod Campbell[139]
This story is simple and direct in its exploration of the consequences of acquiring unsuitable pets. It is funny, but contains an element of realism which produces sighs of relief on the last page when the suitable pet is sent home from the zoo who had, eventually, realised just what was needed. This is an early exploration into the concept of what is reasonable and appropriate and what is not.

Oi, Get Off Our Train[140] by John Burningham
This masterful book deals with environmental issues as different animals are forced from their habitat due to a range of current issues – from deforestation to the killing of animals for their products. This book pulls no punches and although the story is constructed in a magical, dream-like format, it leaves all who read it in no doubt that we need to make changes to our lifestyles to preserve the planet we inhabit.

Just for fun are the nonsensical stories which have children laughing out loud about their impossible consequences:

Don't Let The Pigeon Drive The Bus by Mo Williams[141]
This book explores the possibilities of a world where a bus driver implores the reader to prevent a pigeon from driving his bus while he is away and the pigeon's compelling arguments to be trusted with it. The reader is drawn into the debate as, on every page, the pigeon finds a new and compelling argument for being allowed to drive the bus. Rationally and emotionally, the reader knows they must be strong in resisting the pigeon's appeals, but he is very persuasive!

Ketchup on Your Cornflakes?[142] by Nick Sharratt

This story invites by the reader to make choices about what might taste good with a dressing of a variety of toppings, (talc, toothpaste and custard, to mention just a few).

Although nonsensical, these stories do invite the reader to make decisions based on reasons. This decision-making is contained within the safe framework of fiction and children are offered the experience of knowing what responsible decision-making feels like and having to justify their decisions.

Socially, then, the book area is a wonderful haven of friendship and shared experiences. It is vital that it is available for most of the time children are in the setting, as the processes of getting reacquainted with favourite stories, discovering new ones and trying to make sense from print are not ones that can be hurried. Children need to know that reading can be an *all alone* activity or a shared one. To help with the process of reading itself, books need to be the right size so that children can physically hold them and turn the pages, either on their own or together with a friend. It is for this reason that big books are not always the most appropriate choice: because of their format, they will almost always be used by adults for a large-group time but are hard to maintain in a book corner in good condition.

Talking and reading

The book area is a prime place for learning new language. Stories with repetitive patterns of language such as *Room on the Broom* by Julia Donaldson[143] and *Pass the Jam, Jim* by Kaye Umansky and Margaret Chamberlain[144] will hook children into the sheer delight of trying to get the words in the right order to gain the satisfaction of repeating the lilting rhythms and alliteration used to tell the story. *The Shark in the Park* by Nick Sharrett[145] uses rhyme to give clues as to the meaning in the text and *Don't Forget The Bacon* by Pat Hutchins[146] plays with rhyme by subtly changing the occasional word to alter the meaning entirely. These sound and word games entice children into the story but in so doing teach them the literary possibilities of words and rhymes.

These carefully chosen books will teach children to read by the power of what they have to offer in terms of excitement, comfort, fun and challenge. The practitioner's role is to be there alongside key children to observe and recognise what level they have attained. If a child is at scale point 7 of the Early Years Profile, and is retelling a favourite tale from a book, for example, a practitioner can embed their knowledge by using puppets or by introducing a story sack of the same story so that the child's experience of the sequence of events is varied and deepened. By encouraging a child to guess the last word of a line which rhymes with the line above, the practitioner helps the child to begin to display the reader-like behaviour of gathering meaning from the context surrounding the word to be read. We all do this when faced with a new word and it is the reason that pictures adjoining text must never be hidden from children who use these as clues to decipher meaning. The practitioner's role is to support, extend, encourage and above all, to *enjoy* the book area!

The practitioner's question which relates to the area of social and language development is **'How should we all act towards each other?'**

When considered in terms of the books and stories that will be shared by adults and children, the key element is contained in the last phrase of the above paragraph: both children and adults need to enjoy books and be seen to enjoy books. A culture of literacy will evolve if adults enthusiastically share their favourites not only with the children but also with each other. For new practitioners, the idea of heading straight to the children's section of a library, book shop or charity shop may not come easily and whoever leads the practice may need to model such behaviour by bringing newly discovered gems into the setting and sharing them amongst the adults with obvious delight! All adults working in the setting need to be clear about the definition of 'a good book' in terms of what it offers to children's cognitive, social or emotional development and some staff training time will be well spent in setting the parameters in terms of story, illustrations and text. Individual staff members' favourites should be acknowledged by all and a high profile given to the potential of any new book which has been added to the selection. It may well be worth buying several copies of a favourite book so that the frustration of never being able to read it does not overwhelm the new reader: buying different books by a well-known children's author encourages children to make judgements by saying *'I enjoyed the last one of hers, so I'll try this one'*. A rich literary environment will develop if staff lead the way by encouraging children to talk, give them interesting things to talk about, listen to what children have to say and be creative in their approach to story-making.

The creative area

Creativity is about taking risks and making connections and is strongly linked to play.[147]

This chapter considers those areas of the early years setting where children can make creations, usually of their own design. There is no suggestion that these are the only places in the setting where children or adults are creative because the attitudes of creativity are to be seen in every corner! Because in this book, we are thinking specifically about areas of provision, rather than aspects of the curriculum, the decision was taken to include activities such as painting, picture-making and modelling in this chapter while considering other creative activities such as drawing and constructing in other chapters. Chapter 9 looks at creativity in the graphics area and Chapter 10 looks at creativity in the block area.

This chapter concentrates on what children can create out of open-ended materials rather than prestructured materials because these tend to be the ones that encourage children to think, feel, socialise or concentrate more deeply. They offer opportunities for children to develop in all areas, emotionally, socially, cognitively and physically.

Creativity, as we have seen in other chapters, is the process of making something new out of something that already exists or what the EYFS calls 'transforming understanding'.[148] Essentially creativity is about children following their own designs As we saw in EYFS Card 4.3, creativity is not about 'making a Diwali card just like everyone else's. It is about originality; it goes beyond talent and does not rely on intelligence but on imagination. The creative process consists of both freedoms and controls. There needs to be the 'intellectual freedom to explore ideas, not the freedom to do as you want'[149] alongside controls which are both physical and mental. Making a creation is only possible if children can manipulate the materials they need. Much time and help needs to be built into creative learning so that children know how to use such equipment as a Sellotape dispenser, scissors or glue, and they can gauge how much paper they will need for their painting and learn to mix just the colour they need for their picture. Every creative person needs time to master the 'tools of the trade', and so do children. Mentally, children need to develop the disposition to be creative, which involves cultivating the attitudes of being purposeful and persistent. These life skills are not only necessary if one is going to *make* a creation but also they are developed through the process of *being* creative. In other words, once children are hooked into a creative project by their curiosity, the necessary skills will follow, encouraged by the consistent interest and support of the key person.

The creative area

In a group setting that caters for children from 3 months to 5 years, creative experiences have to be provided for the full age range. The staff are aware that although creativity develops with imagination, their youngest babies will be set on a creative path if given a rich environment that they can begin to interpret through their senses. Within reach of the babies are silk squares, a treasure basket, muslin balls containing herbs for them to squeeze and smell and lots of opportunities for singing and rocking. By providing an atmosphere where babies can begin to anticipate and control events, the necessary aspects of creativity are being recognised and activated. For the mobile babies and young toddlers, there are large sheets of paper where they can sprinkle or throw paint or glue and make marks with their fingers, feet and hands.

For the older children, there is a designated 'messy area', which is where painting, sticking, modelling and the sand and water area are available. The flooring is designed to be mopped down and the children's bathroom is nearby, with easily accessible hand-washing facilities. There are always two types of painting activity on offer, one of which is a permanent fixture. It consists of a range of ready-mixed paints in prime colours and a large paper tub containing a varied selection of different sizes and shapes of paper for painting. Also on the painting table are sharp pencils, so that the finished painting can be named. Nearby is a multilayered rack on which the children can store their paintings to dry.

The other painting table is usually an adult-led activity. It might be printing or perhaps some animals are being painted to make a frieze to accompany a current theme or story. Occasionally, some tie-die may be happening or some self-portraits are being painted. For these more specialist artistic activities, children will experience using different materials such as dyes or powder paints that can be mixed to match tones of skin and hair colour and hues of green for painting outdoor scenes. When this activity takes place, a mirror is positioned nearby, so that self-portrait colours can be checked for accuracy! Children are free to join any of these painting activities whenever there is room. Usually, the more specialist processes seem to be self-limiting, by attracting those children who understand the processes and are curious enough to see the possibilities of what can be achieved and are confident enough to 'have a go'.

Close by the painting tables is a table for model-making, together with a trolley containing easily retrievable materials for making collages or models. This area is known as 'the workshop'. It is available at each session, sometimes with an adult, but often without. The adult's role is to help children with the tricky processes of learning how to use the tools – the scissors, the hole punch, the Sellotape dispenser, the glue and the stapler. By ensuring that children are taught how to use these tools safely, there are very few accidents. Limiting the numbers of children using the area by limiting the number of scissors and glue brushes keeps the area calm and purposeful. Children know that if the workshop is currently too busy for them to have a space, they can return later as it is always available. They can always create whatever they like but sometimes an adult sits in the workshop making his or her own model or is there to come up with some ideas. Currently, some of the children have been making tabards to use as dressing-up clothes. They have asked for large pieces of paper and then drawn around their friends who were lying down on the paper. The pencilled shapes were then cut out and an adult helped to fix some shoulder straps with split pins. The creative delight has been in the drawing, cutting and fixing and not one was decorated in any way. They have been stored by being hung across a drying line and will then be used for imaginative games. Not being too robust, this process will need repeating regularly!

Next to the workshop is a modelling table where there is either clay or play dough. When clay is on offer, an adult is there also, to help with the messy process of experimenting and possibly constructing something. On these days, there will probably not be a specialist painting activity as the staffing levels will not cope with such a high level of support needed. So, painting will be restricted to the permanent table.

Picture-making often happens in the workshop area where children use shiny paper, feathers and sticky shapes to make a collage. On a nearby table, however, is a large piece of hessian. with some blunt bodkins, thread and a selection of buttons, thin pieces of material, pasta, pieces of straws and paper that can sewn onto the hessian. This is a communal activity and stays on the table. Children come and sew something onto the hessian and move on when they have completed their addition. After some weeks there is no more space for additions and an adult makes the finished artwork into a wall hanging. Children remember for a very long time which piece of sewing they completed and are justifiably proud of the joint achievement. Carers and families have to come and inspect which particular button or piece of thread was attached and respond accordingly!

There are opportunities each session, then, for painting, model-making, sewing or threading and junk modelling. Each of these requires a different set of physical skills but all require a disposition towards being creative and having ideas that are the beginning of a process, but not necessarily an end-product. As the EYFS Practice Guidance requires (p 110), this is an area that provides opportunities to 'Explore colour, texture, shape, form and space in two and three dimensions'.[150]

In Chapters 1–4 we considered the theory underpinning children's emotional, physical, social and cognitive development. In this chapter we take those aspects of development in turn and think about how they can be catered for in the creative area of the setting. We also consider the associated practitioner questions.

Children's emotional and behavioural development

The EYFS Practitioner's Guidance tells us that 'Creativity emerges as children become absorbed in action and explorations of their own ideas'.[151]

This phrase 'absorbed in action and exploration of their own ideas' reflects the work of Ferre Laevers.[152] In this work, Laevers summarises the concept of 'involvement', which he states is necessary for deep-level learning, i.e. learning at the edge of a child's

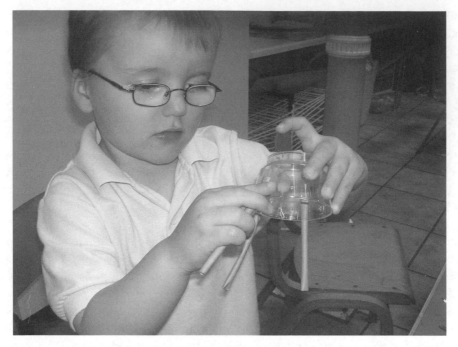

'Involvement is linked directly to children's curiosity and motivation'

capabilities. Involvement is linked directly to children's curiosity and motivation and is evidenced by signals from children, including:

- concentration
- energy
- persistence
- facial expression and posture
- reaction time
- language
- satisfaction.

These observable signals are key indicators of the quality and effectiveness of the learning experience and signify that a good match has been made between the ability and interests of the child and the challenge of the activity. Deep-level learning takes place when it is purposeful and relevant.

Self-esteem

The creative area is one where children can be seen displaying many of Laevers' involvement signals. His signals reflect, not knowledge on its own, but attitudes which derive from how a child feels about the learning they are about to engage with. Clearly, if

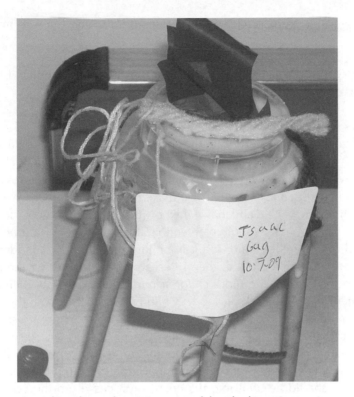

'Deep-level learning takes place when it is purposeful and relevant'

children have a good level of knowledge and understanding of how, for example, paint can be mixed to exactly the colour they need to match the daffodil stems they are painting, this knowledge helps them to feel confident that they can be successful and the other signals will be observable too. Children who believe in their ability to paint a picture of a vase of daffodils will concentrate and be energetic and persistent as they complete the task. Once it is finished, they will feel satisfied and probably will want to talk about their work of art. Creativity, then, depends on the adults' recognising that they need to make this type of activity available on a regular basis so that children can practice and become competent. Practitioners also need to make time to teach children the mechanics of paint-mixing. Creativity is very largely resource-led. Not only will works of art not be forthcoming without the necessary tools but also children will not be drawn to the painting table to practice their skills if it is uninviting because of torn paper, dirty brushes and no clear system of storing work, both completed and work-in-progress. To help a child feel courageous enough to embark on the uncertain business of creating a painting, a clay model or a collage there needs to be:

- an inviting area in which to work with fit-for-purpose resources, enough tools and enough space

- adults available to help with the processes of creating, but not imposing their ideas
- time to complete the project to the child's satisfaction
- a clear system of management of nearly finished and completed work which children can organise themselves.

This last point is sometimes poorly understood in settings. Staff will spend so much time tying aprons, fetching new water for paint mixing and mopping up spillages that they have no time left to talk to children about what they are creating. To build children's self-esteem in this area the adults need to have conversations about the pictures and models. Process conversations such as 'How did you make that greeny colour?' will make children feel their efforts are valued and they will know that the adult is genuinely interested in them and their creations. An adult intervention along the lines of 'Careful, that paint might spill' will, on the other hand, result in children feeling less confident as all the potential disasters are pointed out to them! Research has shown that the more adults used the phrase 'be careful' the more children retreated from experimenting and the fewer involvement signals they displayed.[153] Children who can source their own paper for painting from an accessible store, paint their own picture, name it using their own mark and take it to a known place to dry will be those children whose self-esteem will be high. Very young children and those with particular learning needs will need much greater levels of practical support of course but, nevertheless, opportunities for independence and choice should be built into the creative process from the very start. Those children new to creating can be asked what implements they would like to try, which colour they would like to use and an encouraging dialogue between key person and child will instil those feelings of value that children need to become confident in trying out their ideas.

Positive dispositions

As with many of the areas of the early years setting, it can be seen that *provision*, i.e. open-ended and child-led learning, promotes more in the way of positive dispositions than does *activities,* which tend to have an end-product and be adult led. It cannot be denied that a heavy emphasis on child-led creations leads to much mess and seemingly value-free productions! However, it is vital that opportunities exist for children to learn about the craft of creating, which involves practising how to stick two pieces of cardboard together, and learning that, having applied glue, it is counter-productive to add some Sellotape for good measure! Staff need to make families aware of the stages of learning that have to be gone through along the road to a completed work of art. EYFS Card 4.3 underlines this point by asking practitioners to reflect on whether they 'Give children the experience of playing with paint and glue before expecting them to make a product such as a Christmas card'? It goes without saying that the child faced with a complex, adult-led production to complete will probably lack the disposition to achieve the task as it is not a project that is inside their head, but inside the practitioner's, and without much time allocated to practising skills such as cutting, gluing, painting, threading and sewing, as processes, failure is likely to follow. It is in just this way that a child may well develop the idea that 'I'm not creative', with all the attendant lessening in positive disposition and self-esteem that ensues.

There needs to be a balance, then, between learning that helps children to become proficient in the basic skills of creativity and learning that might have an end-product in which both children and staff can take pride. Children who are familiar with a story such as 'The Very Hungry Caterpillar'[154] will, in all probability, have a positive disposition towards making simple stick puppets to illustrate each of the caterpillar's meals, even though this idea may have been suggested by a practitioner. Guidance is clearly needed here to bring a project such as this to fruition, but the lead practitioner must not feel that, because a large proportion of learning needs to be child-initiated, that the adults in the setting have no role to play except that of enabling and supporting. Of course, these roles are of prime importance, but so too is that of providing a stimulating learning environment and staff who are well trained will be confident to enhance children's learning by suggesting ideas that they know their children will find challenging but achievable and enjoyable.

This is also true of an activity such as the hessian sewing described above. Although the children can choose anything to sew and add to the collage at any time, it was clearly an adult's idea to present this activity in a way that makes it possible for the children to make a successful creative contribution. This sewing project also gives children the possibility of contributing to a joint class venture, and thereby developing a positive disposition to feeling a part of the class effort. As stated earlier, for an activity such as this to be successful, the emphasis must be placed on resourcing and thinking through the way that the activity will be presented. Children need clear rules about the use of bodkins and an adult needs to be responsible for checking that the system is working. The resources need to be presented in a sturdy tray of small compartments and kept muddle-free so that the area can be used with ease. The key features, then, of promoting a positive disposition towards creativity are, firstly, the appropriateness and availability of resources and, secondly, the time to practice creative skills with an adult alongside to help where needed. Adults also need to act as a 'gofer' to make suggestions and supply materials as the project progresses. If these basics are in place, what is likely to follow is enthusiastic creativity with children becoming assured that they are 'can do' people.

Agency

It is in the creative area that children's agency can most successfully be encouraged. 'Agency' has been defined by Roberts [155] as going further than having freedom of choice, as was suggested in Chapter 1. Roberts suggests that it is about developing an internal locus of control, about empowerment, about pride, and about having the ability to influence.[155] In terms of creativity these are immensely useful emotional and behavioural tools to have at one's command when tackling the slippery business of creating something that might well go wrong. One of the major aspects of creativity is that it is a risky process and can all so easily end in failure. Young children will inevitably see any such failure as theirs and this is precisely where a key person can play such a valuable role by talking through a project, suggesting possible ways through a problem and having enough knowledge of the child to recognise when the creation is complete in the child's eyes.

A high internal locus of control, which is a key feature of agency, will give a child the belief that her ideas are as valuable as anyone else's. She will believe that any success is as a result of her own efforts. She is thus in a position to take responsibility for her learning and is in a position to influence other children who will recognise her confidence and pride. When expecting children to make creations, this issue of locus of control is of prime importance. In order to foster attitudes of pride, confidence and autonomy in children, it is counter-productive to give them templates to draw around or to present, for example, a house shape which is square with a triangle for a roof. These types of interactions give out the very powerful message to children that their ideas are not valid and it is the adult who knows the right way to paint animals or houses. My experience of teaching very young children bears out this fact. When asked to paint a house, children will very often paint a picture of their bedroom because it is the most important aspect of their home. They will then be happy to discuss all the contents, including their favourite toys, whereas they are unlikely to have much to say about a square house with a triangle roof which probably looks nothing like their home. A consistent message to children that they are unable to create without adults providing templates or trimming around the edges will soon discourage them from 'having a go', as well as shifting the children's locus of control from internal to external, where children are constantly aiming to please the adults rather than themselves. Instead of the agency and autonomy that we as practitioners should be enabling, we will find that our children will become ever more dependent and ever more likely to say 'I can't do that'.

Belonging and boundaries

In the area where children can express themselves freely, each individual child must feel that they have ways of self-expression that feel right for them. EYFS Card 1.2 states that effective practice will 'encourage a child to recognise their own unique qualities and the characteristics that they share with other children'.[156] This sense that individuality is celebrated and that this uniqueness contributes to the richness of the setting lies at the heart of believing that one 'belongs'. Creative opportunities must reflect the differences that children will have, in abilities, in cultures, in preferences and in needs. A feeling that a child has that they truly belong to the setting is to do with a sense of identity, security and trust. A sense of identity will be enhanced if, for example, natural materials which are brought in as an inspiration for art work, reflect the lived lives of the children and reflect their cultures. Security will be fostered if the key person is genuinely knowledgeable about children's families. Using this knowledge, each of their children's temperaments and preferences can be matched to creative tasks that are appropriate for each child.

The trust that is then built up will be the vehicle through which the child will be encouraged to try something as yet untried. The joy of the caring adult in seeing the child's success is hugely important, as is the comfort and support when things do not go so well.

Alongside the feelings of acceptance and belonging come the boundaries; the expectations, the rules and the responsibilities that we considered in Chapter 1. Applied to the area in the setting where children are going to be creative, they become a mainstay in protecting children's vulnerability as they experiment and explore new materials and try out new ideas. Tools and equipments need to be carefully used and stored and other people's work to be treated with respect. Adults are sometimes more guilty than the children of destroying creations that are 'too large' or 'in the way'. Deep and genuine distress is caused to children's slender sense of creative worth when they see their creations, over which they have spent much time and commitment, being packed away or stowed out of reach on a high, dusty shelf. Systems need to be put in place so that children's models, painting, threadings and the like can be placed, preferably by the children themselves, somewhere where they can be retrieved at group time or home time and shared with friends and family. In fact, by putting the child's sense of belonging at the forefront of practice in such seemingly minor ways, practitioners will be able to see the nursery experience though the eyes of the children. Adults will recognise that how they organise routines and storage and how they promote the use of resources is crucial to each child's view of themselves. These feelings of self-worth or worthlessness have, in their turn, huge implications for children's emotional and behavioural development.

So, 'How should children feel about themselves and their learning in the creative area?'

When children are painting, modelling, threading, sewing or engaged in any truly creative activity they will feel as if they are working hard. This is because they will be fully engaged in their project and will be devoting time, energy and precision in their concentrated efforts to achieve their goal. However, it would be more accurate to suggest that, although they are applying all their skills and knowledge to their task, they are in fact using a playful approach. This is because there may well be no fixed outcome, no set way to proceed and no time limit; the only driving force is the child's intention. This is a rather 'loose' way of learning, as opposed to 'tight' learning, which involves measurable outcomes and right or wrong answers. As such, it lies at the centre of creativity, as it reveals what children are thinking. In his poem 'The Hundred Languages of Children', Loris Malaguzzi uses the phrase 'They tell the child to think without hands and to do without head',[157] suggesting that, in reality, the way children reveal their thoughts is through their creative actions and that to create something worthwhile requires a lot of thinking. Children will therefore feel that they are working hard; however, it will be a pleasurable feeling because they are in control of the creative process. The process of making decisions about design and how to execute the design is a truly complex one and this is where their confidence may founder if a key person is not on hand to encourage and support. Once completed, the child feels enormous pride in his achievements and will often show this by wanting to talk though what he has created with a friend or an adult.

Children's cognitive and intellectual development

When observing children making and painting, adults will notice that their actions are rarely random. Although not necessarily leading to a recognisable conclusion, children will be bringing what they know and can do to their actions. A child may well not know what his painting will look like when it is finished, but so it is with adults' creativity. A creation evolves during the process of production and the creator will constantly be evaluating, making changes and trying out new ideas. These mental processes of prediction, evaluation, adjustment and reflection are high-order thought processes which are a necessary part of making a creation worthwhile and valuable. Even if, as in the case of a young child, the end result is a sawn-off piece of wood with a hole in it, this represents perhaps an hour of this high-order thinking. For this length of time the child has been concentrating on carrying an intention in her head: speculating what she might try doing, selecting the necessary tools, struggling with equipment and persisting when the task seemed impossible. It is this struggle that is poorly rewarded when the piece of wood is disregarded and treated as valueless. It is because of this response that children become so upset when their creations are not recognised as representing the effort and commitment that they have given to them.

Learning new knowledge

During the process of creating, children will gather vast quantities of new knowledge. Take, for example, the child painting a self-portrait. There are two kinds of knowledge involved here: one of them involves the process of production ('*How do I mix the right colour paint to match my skin*'?) the other is the aesthetic element ('*What will my creation look like when it is finished, and indeed, when will it be finished? Will I be pleased with it, will it look like me*'?).The first element is objective in nature and skills based; the second is far more subjective, affective and emotive.

A venture such as the self-portrait not only gives a message to each child that their uniqueness is to be celebrated but also gives children the opportunity to consider in depth, perhaps for the first time, the concept that everyone looks different. The thinking skills of observation, classification, comparison, analysis and reason are put to good use in a project such as this. As well as these purely cognitive skills, the project offers children the opportunity to develop understandings, and to consider concepts such as causality and diversity. In some creative activities there is also the element of representing an experience and perhaps expressing an emotion. The understanding that feelings and experiences can be represented creatively gives children a powerful way of dealing with new and partly understood ideas. Through their creativity they come to know that as well the *things* that are all around them, there are *ideas* as well and that they can be in control of how these ideas are explored and expressed. The skill they will need above all others to investigate these ideas creatively is imagination. When the ability to imagine is well developed, children will be able to use their understanding of symbolic representation to invent and weave ideas for their own purposes. Unlike the symbolic representation of print where everyone uses the same system – i.e. the written word *BALL* is the universal way in which a ball is represented in the English language – through creativity, there are an infinite number of ways to represent both objects and ideas. The sole constraint is a creator's imagination! A flower, a wedding, a friend or a concept such as circles or the dark can be represented in a myriad of different ways and children have the freedom to choose the way that is most meaningful for them. This is exactly what Loris Malaguzzi meant when he wrote the poem *The Hundred Languages of Children*.[158]

Schemas

Schematic play in young children is a powerful method of nourishing and supporting their growing understanding of a concept. We considered the part that schemas play in helping children to securely embed a concept that they are learning about in Chapter 1. The creative area is rich in opportunities for children to enter into this process by allowing them to play, experiment and explore in ways of their choosing, thus enabling them to use the creative materials that are available to become more certain about newly encountered concepts. Think, for example, about a young child whose attention is drawn to the idea of how things are joined together. Called the 'connecting' schema, the child's attention is first drawn to the process of how different things are connected: it intrigues her. Consider that she must understand that the Brio train track is joined together differently from how the pages of a book are joined together or from how tying a piece of string can join things together. The only way that children can learn these concepts is by trying them out. With the glue, Sellotape, split pins and staplers at her disposal in the creative area there are many rich opportunities for her to experiment and learn about how things join together. The child is likely to become somewhat obsessive in her play because she needs to practice these processes again and again until she is completely sure that she has the concepts securely understood. The important aspects for the practitioner to realise is that, first, the child will not be likely to be able to offer a rational explanation as to why she is always playing in this way and, secondly, that the learning is about the process of joining and not about making an end-product, Hence, there will be much Brio track joined together but no train ever added, pieces of cardboard stuck in various ways with no finished model and much fumbling with string without necessarily any visible purpose except the process of tying itself.

As the child becomes sure that she has understood the concept of joining, practitioners, in their observations, will note that the schematic play lessens and finally stops but that she is now competent at using the tools and toys in the setting to play her way. She has embedded the concept, in her mind, needs no more external practice but has taken ownership of the concept, which enables her to use it confidently and for her purposes. The schemas that are most apparent in the creative area are 'enveloping and containing', as children fill small boxes with the contents of the workshop; 'rotation', as they paint circular patterns and pictures; and 'covering', where they can be observed painting a beautiful picture and then covering it all in black paint! The practitioner's role here is to understand and recognise this aspect of children's development, which is a powerful tool in their understanding of basic concepts, and when they have recognised it, support it and provide the environment which will enable the children to follow their particular leaning pattern for as long as it is needed.

The practitioner's question associated with children's cognitive and intellectual development in the creative area is: **'How do I know where children are in their learning and how can I move them on?'**
The EYFS is helpful in stating what we as educators are aiming for in the ways we move children's learning forward as they become increasingly creative. It talks specifically about children 'initiating their own learning' and how practitioners must 'give sufficient time for children to explore and develop ideas and finish working through these ideas'. There is the encouragement to provide a 'stimulating environment', one in which 'creativity, originality and expressiveness are valued'. The phrase 'a stimulating environment' does not always paint a clear enough picture in practitioners' minds but should encompass the two key aspects of creativity, which are – the *processes* necessary to create and the business of invention. In other words, the area needs to be clear in its intention so that scissors can be found, brushes are clean and attractive and children know what to do with finished work. Then there is the motivation to create something original in the workshop or at the easel. The area needs to be presented in such a way as to invite the child in. As a rule of thumb, if the practitioner finds the area inviting, so, too, will the child.

Our knowledge of children's development will inform us of what we would expect to see in terms of creativity. We would like to see children developing competence at manipulating tools and understanding the nature of and uses for paint, paste, glue and any other modelling materials offered to them for exploration. We would like to see children learn about colour, about texture, tone, form and shape. But above all, we know that children have the potential to respond to stimulation with enthusiasm and wonder and that, by concentrating on things that are interesting and meaningful to them, they can create new meanings and ideas from the materials they are offered. Consistent opportunities to see, feel and use a rich range of materials will encourage competence in the ability to use tools and materials to serve their purposes and loving support will encourage responses which will be unique and often astonishing in their originality and complexity. It is by observing, by listening and by interacting that staff will be able to assess with confidence their key children's levels of creativity and by open-ended questioning that they will succeed in suggesting how deeper and more considered thought will lead to ever more imaginative creations.

Creative expression gives practitioners good opportunities to use language that accompanies the processes involved in painting and model making. As there is a large sensory component to this area of the curriculum, practitioners can ask questions and make comments such as '*Is it a pale enough green*'? , *What do you think that dough smells of*?' and '*I love your bright red splatter pattern!*'. These comments give children encouragement that their efforts are important to their key adults. It gives them language to use to describe their actions as well as challenging them to think more deeply about what they are doing. Children's learning will be moved on if they are given language to accompany their creative play as they gain increased confidence to ask for what they need, 'I'd like the thinner/fatter brush, please', and talk through with a friend or adult their work, 'My clay feels really squidgy'.

Physical and motor development

As we saw in Chapter 3, 'the mind is fed by information that the body submits to it'.[159] The two are completely intertwined and so the more opportunities children have to develop their physical prowess, particularly in their fine manipulative skills, the more ambitious will be their creative designs as they know that they are capable of using the equipment they need to be creative. For example, most settings recognise the skill of threading is one that adds to children's range of manipulative abilities. Sewing, such as the activity described above, also gives children opportunities to practice, at their own level, a set of skills that may well be needed when being creative. Sometimes these activities are not presented in open-ended ways that accord with the idea of making creations. There are many rather stereotyped threading boards and laces being over-looked by children in settings who do not see the activity as a particularly attractive one, as it carries little meaning for the child. Better, perhaps, to supply children with pieces of card and a hole punch and let them design their own patterns of holes. There will be much more enthusiasm and commitment then to joining up the holes by threading a lace or piece of wool through them, as it is (in the child's mind) an original design. Similarly, weaving can greatly increase children's fine manipulative skills but needs to be pre-sented as an open-ended, perhaps whole-group activity, that can be added to whenever the child feels so inclined. A garden cone, the sort sold in garden centres to support plants, made from wicker, works very well for this purpose, with children having no shortage of ideas as to what could be used to weave through it! These examples give sug-gestions of ways that children's physical skills can be developed without the stress associated with possible failure or boredom. The more practice and success children can have, the more enthusiastically and confidently they will approach the business of using their abilities to create something new.

It is also recognised that children who show the most dexterity and confidence in using their fine motor skills for creative reasons as well as to write are those who have had good previous experiences with practising large, or gross, motor skills. Very young children, particularly toddlers, need creative experiences which are large in scale and with no end-product as the purpose of the activity is the sensory experience of feeling the play dough between the fingers, or better still, smelling if it has been laced with lavender oil, and watching the result of splattering paint on a huge piece of paper. It is by experi-encing these early open-ended physical creative processes that babies and toddlers will develop a love of creating, which is born of an emerging confidence in their abilities to create something worthwhile.

'How can I ensure that resources are available for children to use actively and independently?'

Successful creativity is largely resource-driven. There are several key aspects to providing resources that are vital to consider if children are to feel empowered to have a go at making something new from the resources that are available. These are:

- A working environment that is well-organised. Resources need to be fit for purpose, though not necessarily expensive, and regularly maintained. They need to be easy for children to access by themselves and consistently kept in the same place so that children can remember from where to fetch and return them. Protective clothing needs to be chosen so that children can use it independently: perhaps a tabard design with Velcro fastenings and plastic sleeve protectors with elastic that can be easily pulled on and off. Conversations between adults and children will thus be able to be focused on the creating process or the creation rather than the lower-level management conversations about doing-up aprons and mopping-up spillages.

- A variety of resources so that children can make realistic choices about what they need in order to make their creation. This means paper and card of various sizes, shapes and colours, paint brushes of different widths, right- and left-handed scissors, a selection of tools to print with, pattern makers and rollers. There should be natural materials to add to the dough such as twigs, feathers and shells. The workshop area should contain a range of threads such as wool, cotton, string and ribbons as well as differently shaped small boxes, cardboard tubes and straws, corks and bottle tops. This is what is meant by a 'stimulating environment' and will give children lots of ideas as to how to use these types of resources to explore their creative possibilities.

- How resources are used is a crucial element in planning the creative environment. If practitioners fully understand that children, or in fact anyone, cannot create in a hurry, they will build in as much time as possible, without a break, for creative resources to be available so that children's ideas can go through the necessary incubating process.

- Adults need to be nearby while creating is happening. Sometimes they will need to offer the occasional practical suggestion, sometimes they will need to observe from a distance and sometimes they will need to be a 'creative partner', being alongside the new or vulnerable creator as they make tentative steps in asserting their individuality and originality.

- Photos of recently created painting, models and collages which are displayed in the creative area will give children who are new to this process some ideas as to what is possible. Photos also generate conversations and children will spend considerable amounts of time talking about the photos of their work to their friends and to staff. Photos that have been taken during the creating process are immensely valuable as they value the unfinished child's product and emphasise that it is the process that is just as creative as the finished model or painting. These photos also record the sequence of events that led up to the finished product and which help children become more secure in the concept of 'What happened first and what happened next'.

- The EYFS reminds us that children can be inspired by beautiful works of art in just the same way that we can as adults.[160] (Practice Guidance p 107). These can range from prints of great paintings (Van Gogh's 'Sunflowers' often inspires young painters I have found, particularly if timed to coincide with the planting and measuring of sunflower seeds in the setting's garden!) sculptures and music to natural materials (such as pieces of driftwood or a richly patterned piece of material), and will all in their different ways offer starting points for children's imagination as they seek ways to represent what they have experienced in looking at and perhaps feeling from examples of other peoples' responses to experiences.

Social and language development

Painting, collage and model making are powerful ways for children to represent their experiences of the world around them. A shared experience which might have been inspired by a favourite book or fairy story will often draw in many children as they can all share in the emotions of the plot that they already know well. A book such as John Burningham's 'Oi, Get Off Our Train'[161] gives opportunities for children to paint the animals who are asking to be allowed to get on the train. If the book has captured their imagination there will be no shortage of children eager to represent the animals, which can then be assembled into a frieze along with the train. If the frieze is displayed at child height, they can add to it and it will become the centre of many conversations relating to the story. Practitioners may also find that animals not in the original story will find their way into the group picture, a signal that real creativity is thriving in the setting! A cooperative venture such as this, and the hessian sewing or the weaving mentioned above, are powerful in their inclusivity. They value each child's unique contribution and allow all the children to feel that they have something valuable to offer. They can thus contribute at a level which is developmentally appropriate for them and feel proud of their contribution. A young child will often bring a parent or a friend to the picture that she has added and say, with justifiable pride, 'I did that!' Developmentally, what is important here is that there are many acceptable levels of connection with an activity such as this. Margaret Carr, in her work on learning stories,[162] used five different dispositions of learning and used staff's observations of children showing these dispositions to assess where they were in their learning journey. The five dispositions are:

- taking an interest
- being involved
- persisting with difficulty or uncertainty
- expressing an idea or feeling
- taking responsibility.

Margaret Carr suggests that the youngest learners or those at the earliest stages of experiencing a group creative piece such as the displayed frieze will be at the stage of 'taking an interest', perhaps walking up to the picture and looking at it or touching it. The child who is rather more familiar with it will become involved, perhaps by talking about it to a friend or contributing an animal to the picture. From there it is a short step to becoming so committed to contributing to the picture that even when cutting the elephant shape seems daunting or the right colour for the camel is almost impossible to mix, the child struggles on until a solution is reached. By talking through their ideas of what should be in the picture or by joining a group discussion about the message of the book, that of global warming, a child shows that they are at the stage of 'expressing an idea or feeling'. The final disposition would be in evidence when a child begins to take responsibility for the picture, suggesting new ideas, helping to maintain it and assisting other children to make their contributions.

As well as allowing children to engage with an activity at an appropriate developmental stage for them individually, this type of cooperative learning provides opportunities for staff to assess children within a sociocultural context: i.e. within the normal ongoing activities of the setting. This will give more accurate results, and higher results than more external, formal assessment tools, as children are going about their normal playful activities and have the motivation to achieve at their highest levels.

As Carr also states, learning in this way enables children to think more deeply, more widely and for longer as they take the opportunities offered to adapt the story to their own ends. They will discover that, in this open-ended environment, they can think about possible additions to the picture and debate – perhaps, the wisdom of inviting a hungry crocodile to board the train! As the debate grows, so does the rich language that accompanies the production of the train, the track, the snowscape, the fog and the animals.

It is not, of course, just in cooperative artistic projects such as this that assessment opportunities arise, but in setting up provision and activities that children can use together and in their own, negotiated ways, and practitioners will discover the truism that Vygotsky gave us, that learning is, in essence, a social activity. The preschools of Reggio Emilia in Northern Italy work on just this principle: that creative ideas need to be planned, discussed, fine-tuned and some aspects of them rejected before the most universally acceptable version is realised. The social skills and the language that this type of process demands are complex and sophisticated and will take a long time to put in place in the setting but the effort is well worth it as practitioners see children developing in the basic 'super skills' of learning which, as we have seen, are 'motivation, social skills and self-confidence'.[163] We saw in Chapter 4 that the children's social development follows a pattern in which they develop their perception of themselves, their relationships with others and their relationship to the environment. Joint, open-ended, group activities which involve planning, discussion, making choices and coping with adapting the original idea are powerful in giving children practice in these life skills.

The practitioner's question in response to this aspect of children's development is '**How should we all act towards each other?**'.

A response might be found in the title of this book: i.e. that we should be 'responsive' towards one another and, thus, towards one another's creative ideas. One of the other lessons to be learned from the preschools in Reggio Emilia is that they have dispensed with the pedagogy of 'the teacher' and 'the learner'. In these schools, the adult and the child co-construct meaning together towards a conclusion that is unknown to either while the process of creating is continuing. Although it is unwise to suggest that a culturally based system of education can be transferred to another culture, there are lessons to be learned from the notion that children's ideas are just as valuable as the adults' and should be considered with the same respect. Adults can model this respect in their actions and attitudes towards each other. The atmosphere that is promoted through this mutual respect is evident to the children, who feel nurtured and valued. This nurturing atmosphere, in its turn, gives them the confidence to try out new, untested ideas in the knowledge that it is their efforts that will be rewarded and not their performance. All children and adults in the setting need to know with certainty that their suggestions are taken seriously, their shortcomings are understood and their strengths are celebrated.

Role play and the imagination

8

Imagination has been defined as a process in which the individual 'contemplates what is not, but might be'.[164] Imagination happens in the mind; it could be called play that has not yet seen action. Its value, as Einstein reminds us, is that, as a function, 'logic will take you from A to B, imagination will take you everywhere'.

This chapter will consider how a child's development is enhanced by the imaginative play that happens during their role-play experiences. It is important to acknowledge that children's imagination is sparked in many areas of the setting, particularly if the setting has, as part of its pedagogy, the understanding that *'feeling'* is as important as *'knowing'*. Children and adults will have imaginative ideas in the sand, in the construction area, in the music area and when they write and draw, but because we are thinking about the setting through the different areas that are provided for children, the role-play area will be the focus of this discussion.

It might be helpful at this point to clarify a few ideas about the nature of imagination as it happens in early years education.

- To imagine, the player needs to be able to suspend disbelief: i.e. believe that what is being played is, for the length of the game, real.
- The player needs to be able to combine what they know with what they feel. It is this meeting of thinking and feeling that is the stuff of rich imaginative scenarios.
- The imaginative player also needs to understand and use the concept of symbolism and be confident in using one thing to represent something else.
- We know that 2-year-old children who regularly role play develop into emotionally aware adults.[165]
- We know the scenarios played out in the role-play area represent both shared knowledge and individual experiences.

A role-play area

An early years setting in the centre of a Midlands city is situated within a 5-minute walk of one of two major rivers that run through the city centre. As the city is a major tourist venue, small boats constantly travel along the river in the summer months taking tourists

'Scenarios ... represent both shared knowledge and individual experiences'

to see views of the city from the river bank and to go further down the river to visit a nearby town. A small group of the nursery's children had been taken by practitioners on such a trip and had returned to nursery full of tales of their journey.

To follow up this outing, staff discussed with all the children what might be needed to set up a role-play area to reflect their boat trip. Despite the fact that only a handful of children had been on the visit, most of them lived around the river and so had everyday experiences of walking along the tow path and seeing the tourist boats passing by.

The discussion in the small-group times elicited some expected and some unexpected requests. The consensus was for an area in the nursery that could be turned into a 'quay' where they paid for their ticket and boarded the boat. Expected props that the children knew they would need were life jackets, cameras, picnics, bread for the ducks, tickets, a uniform for the boatman, a small set of oars for emergencies and money. Less predictable was the suggestion that they needed a large map of the journey. One of these had been seen by the children at the boarding point and each child had received a pamphlet with a map together with their ticket. It was decided to paint a large, poster-style map of the journey, which would include all the sights of interest along the way. This would be placed at child-height on the wall in the role-play area and so could be added to when necessary. This part of the project proved unexpectedly popular as children who did not go on the trip, but who knew about the river bank, began to draw ducks, park benches and, in some cases, their own houses and friends to add to the landscape.

A generous amount of space was allocated in one corner of the nursery and in the first instance the walls were decorated with posters. These were gradually replaced by the children's own paintings as they became more familiar with the boating experience and became ever more enthusiastic about painting the churches, houses, boats and birds that can be seen from the river banks. Stories and books such as 'The Wind in the Willows',[166] 'Who Sank the Boat?'[167] and 'Mr Gumpy's Outing'[168] helped to provide pictures of what could be seen near the river and the stories gave children a feel for possible plots, many of them involving sinking!

The necessary equipment was installed with the help of parents who had been told of the project. A large bench became the 'boat'; this gave the height necessary for children to row in case of malfunctioning engines. Storage racks were placed next to the bench to hold the life jackets and provide space for cameras and picnics. A ticket office, with a chair and a desk, was arranged next to the boat and children had to state their destination and offer a fare in return for a ticket. The ticket officer had to wear a hat to identify his role and the boatman wore a jacket and a hat. All 'passengers' had to wear life jackets and this provided a helpful way of regulating numbers.

On the day that 'River Tours' opened for business, the enthusiasm was overwhelming. Anticipating this, the staff had planned for an adult to be the ticket officer initially to model the role and some of the possible play scenarios for the children. She asked the passengers where they were going, issued tickets, sometimes with the destination written on them and took the ticket money, placing it in the till. She helped the children 'climb' onto the boat and announced when the boat was full. She modelled language that the children might need in their games and showed them very clearly the rules and expectations of the area. Although this may sound constraining to children's imagination, it is in fact a key feature of good practice in new role-play projects as very young children need to be able to join the play at a range of levels and will not often be able to construct sophisticated play scenarios at the outset. There should be opportunities for children to try 'buying a ticket', 'rowing', 'taking pictures', 'feeding the ducks' and generally getting a feel for being in role on the boat before they can engage in complex role-play adventures. Just as in other forms of learning, much practice has to take place before a high level of imaginative learning can be expected. A chaotic role-play area will not afford the imaginative opportunities that might have been hoped for and will degenerate into a place that is unattractive, unruly and even frightening for the inexperienced player. Role play is an area which, in order to give free range to the imagination, has to operate within a set of rules that are agreed to and adhered to by all players. It is because children will need to be able to use the area in a range of ways and at different levels of understanding that it needs to have as much space as possible and as much time as possible. There must be room and time for a group of players to invent complex scenarios as well as for the player who needs to practice climbing in and out of the boat. If an area such as this is to be truly inclusive and to cater for children's cognitive, emotional, physical and social developmental needs, much care needs be taken at the planning stage to ensure effective implementation.

As the children began to understand the possible roles and adventures more clearly, the adult began to withdraw, adopting an observing role (which changed to an intervening one if the play was seen to need support). As the days went on, adults monitored the use of the area, suggesting different plots and adding new props as needed to enrich the quality of the imaginative play. 'River Tours' remained a well-used role-play area for many weeks and inspired an outdoors version which children created themselves using milk crates as well as an indoor water activity where a range of small boats, powered in different ways, were raced along its length.

In Chapters 1–4 we considered the theory underpinning children's emotional, physical, social and cognitive development. In this chapter we will take those aspects of development in turn and think about how they can be catered for in the role-play area of the setting. We will also consider the associated practitioner questions.

Children's emotional and behavioural development

The major strength of a role-play area, such as the one described above, is that it has an immediate connection with the children who come to the nursery. The river touches everyone's lives and, thus, every child feels that the area is relevant to them. In terms of emotional development, children feel that they understand what a river is and, because they see it most of the days, they have a connection with it and feel empowered to add something to the map or make a suggestion for play plots. Central to successful learning in the early years is to ensure that the planned learning has genuine meaning for the child. Children need considerable exposure to the sights, smells, sounds and atmosphere of the river before they can be expected to represent their river experiences in imaginative play, paintings or drawings. Only when they feel confident and secure in their understandings can they offer a contribution from their imagination to add to the general fund of knowledge and interpretations. It is, however, the contributions that they make, when sensitively received and responded to, that give children the confidence that comes from having their ideas valued and acted upon. Yes, there will be crocodiles and dinosaurs in the river and many near-sinking disasters, but imagination is all about suspending disbelief! Practitioners have a golden opportunity when supporting children's role play, to help them develop plot lines, however unrealistic they may seem, for this is the process by which they try out new ideas, some of which are rejected and some of which are picked up by others and become favourites to be played and replayed with increasing sophistication.

Self-esteem

For children to feel able to both gain from and offer something worthwhile to a role-play area, practitioners need to be aware of the wide range of children's developmental needs. In practical terms it may be that it is just not possible to incorporate the 2 year olds into an area where older players are setting off down a river in the jungle equipped with a well-rehearsed and carefully thought-through script. Often it is good practice to arrange a separate area for these younger children and those with a less well-developed sense of plot.

This, less-demanding area, can be a simple den where one can just 'be' rather than having to be in role. For children who find complex imaginative play too challenging, a den can provide a valuable experience in being somewhere different. If there are hand-bags, hats, wigs or small puppets around in the den, the new player has the chance to try out some imaginary ideas in a less public environment: a safe place which offers containment and feels comforting. In providing props for children to experiment with, staff encourage the development of the imagination and, by being alongside the very young as they begin to put their imagination into actions and become creative in their play, adults give the children the message that what they are doing is a valuable activity and one which has adult support and approval. As current research helps us to understand, learning at children's very early stages *is* the raising of self-esteem through a loving key-person relationship. It is this that gives newly imaginative players the confidence to try out and practice their ideas. In particular, and when supported by a key person, props linked to well-known stories can provide a platform for a toddler to begin imagining. In her book, *'In Mrs Tulley's Room: A Childcare Portrait'*, [169] Vivian Gussin Paley reports 2-year-old children 'doing stories' as they interpret well-known plots with adult help. In their work on early imaginative thought, Julia Manning-Morton and Maggie Thorp remind us that

> Where there are high quality opportunities for babies and toddlers to create and image…the key person is attentive to a child's creative explorations, providing assistance in a way that does not disrupt the child's flow of thinking and through their unobtrusive support gives the child the emotional security to experiment.[170]

Agency

We have seen, in Chapter 1, that 'agency' is a feeling that an individual has some control, influence and freedom of choice over one's actions. It is in genuinely child-centred play that children can most easily feel that they are in control over what is happening because they, not the adults, have made decisions about such aspects as the direction their play will take, who will be the actors and what props will be needed. Tina Bruce states that 'This sense of control impinges upon self-esteem, self-confidence, autonomy, intrinsic motivation, the desire to have a go, to take risks and to solve problems and the ability to make decisions and to choose'.[171] This list of the attributes of 'a sense of control' is deeply impressive and should make us aware of the necessity of handing as much control to children as we realistically can in order to enable them to benefit from the 'can-do' attitudes listed above. In reality, of course, control is a balancing affair and, as we noted in the scenario above, the adults need, at least at first, to have control of the management of complex role-play areas and to establish the boundaries and rules. These rules, having been agreed with the children, are seen to protect the freedom to play in ordered and organised ways. Planned and organised role-play areas enable children to express their imaginative ideas in ways that would be impossible in a chaotic environment. The rules are negotiable: they can be altered, kept, or new ones are created as the need arises. This flexibility allows children to influence the rules and to see the role-play possibilities 'in the round' and from other children's points of view. In fact, the business of setting, agreeing and adjusting rules or boundaries to the play replicates the process to be seen in a democracy and is vital in supporting children's sense of agency. The understanding that children can influence the course of events is empowering and enhances all children's feelings of belonging. It is through this truly democratic process that children will feel that they have ownership of their role-play area, which will encourage their desire to play there and to devise ever more intricate and deeply thought-through plots.

The role-play area is a place where control by the player is more easily established than in other areas of provision. This is because dramatic play at this level rarely has an end-product. In much of the daily provision and activities within a setting adult influence can impinge on and stifle true imagination and creativity but role play, with its emphasis on 'as if' and 'what if?' only functions successfully if players uses their own imagination and control to test the feelings associated with new or challenging ideas. The power of such play lies in the fact that children can be, as Vygotsky remarked, 'a head taller than themselves' and, in doing so, can become engaged in a struggle that demands all their powers of concentration, decision-making and problem-solving. An example of this was noted in the role-play scenario described above, when, during one trip down the river, the boat took a wrong turn and was threatened by a weir. The children, none of whom who had, thankfully, ever been in this situation, were not imitating the impending catastrophe but recreating it. It was clearly not 'pretending' but 'being', as they struggled with all their might to row to safety and save their boat. They were employing all that they knew, all that they felt and all that they could do in the task they had set themselves and it was a mammoth struggle indeed.

Children will also recreate stressful experiences that they have experienced, such as a visit to a hospital, moving house, or the birth of a sibling. Imaginative role play, in a safe environment, will help children to have another look at what has happened to them and they may well need to have repeated opportunities to examine the event before being able to take ownership of it and deal with it. In water play, for example, a 4-year-old boy can bath a doll as if it was his new baby brother and thus gain some sense of agency over the new feeling of being 'an older brother', which emotionally is a huge step from being an only child. In this type of role play he can try being gentle, or not so gentle, with his new brother and safely explore some difficult feelings. A responsive practitioner will know about this family event and be sensitive to his need to have access to imaginative play experiences that will help him to work through a clash of feelings and be on hand to talk to him, if appropriate, about his play and his conflicting emotions.

The practitioner's question in relation to children's emotional and behavioural development in the role-play area is '**How should children feel about themselves and their learning?'**

Children who are engaged in dramatic play often find themselves in uncharted emotional territory. It is the place where they face their fears in real life as we saw above, and where they imagine adventures that they would be unlikely to encounter in reality. Strong emotions are often aroused and this is why the role-play areas, both inside and out, are often seen as difficult for staff to manage. As the play becomes noisier and less predictable, far from seeing the children as in control of their imaginative experiences, practitioners tend to see them as out of control: or rather, out of the adult's control. This does present a challenge to some staff, particularly those who lack confidence or experience themselves and feel that anything other than 'calm and thoughtful' is not worthwhile play. It is also difficult to defend play that develops along the 'rough and tumble' route to other adults and parents, as it will quickly be interpreted as 'playing about' rather than 'playing' and therefore of lesser value. It is necessary to be an advocate for the full range of children's play and to explain that all worthwhile dramatic role play carries with it deep emotions and that the great dramas of our culture such as Macbeth or, indeed, Snow White, would not be fulfilling their cathartic emotional function if they were completely 'calm and thoughtful'! Of course, adults need to be responsible for the quality of learning in the role-play area as in all areas of the setting and need to ensure that children are safe and not disrupting other learners. It may be that the outside is a more suitable venue for such highly charged play and that an adult is on hand to ensure that the plot has meaning. I have often found that a gentle question along the lines of '*I don't quite understand what is happening in this game. Can you tell me what happens next?*' is enough to draw the game back on track and to remind the players that a plot is an expectation and that an adult is around to monitor and raise the level of the play if necessary. In their role play children should feel emotionally safe, although they will often be emotionally challenged, and they also need to know that their ideas and feelings are respected and valued. They should feel that have ownership over at least some aspects of the game and that they have a voice in the negotiated script. They should all feel that they belong to the joint project and also that it has meaning for them individually. As much emotion and effort is invested in this type of play, children will feel a huge sense of satisfaction and increased confidence as a result of playing above their capabilities, whether, for example, they are rescuing the threatened boat or successfully bathing the baby. They may feel excited or exhausted, or both, and may well need some time and opportunity to talk about their role play or to look through books that deal with similar scenarios. Some 'downtime' often follows animated play as children embed these powerful emotional experiences securely into their minds. High-quality dramatic play will help children feel more confident, more autonomous, and able to make more decisions and choices in their everyday lives as they try out and internalise these emotions in their role play.

Children's cognitive and intellectual development

If role play is one of the most powerful tools that practitioners have in developing children's emotional development, it can be argued that it is no less effective in providing riches for children's cognitive development as well. As a headteacher, I was sometimes asked by parents to encourage their children to 'move on' from the domestic role-play area as it was seen as limiting to their intellectual development. In response to this, I included a full page in the school brochure of the learning that was possible from a well-managed and resourced home-play area. In this, I suggested that children could learn the following things within the framework of the Early Years Foundation Stage Curriculum:

Knowledge and understanding of the world:
 daily family routines, their own and others
 cooking familiar and unfamiliar food
 using usual and unusual cutlery
 clothing, both familiar and different and make believe
 celebrations, known and those of other cultures
 relationships between siblings, different generations, pets and toys
 physical properties of packets, bowls, liquids and equipment

Communication, language and literacy:
 acting in role as family members and friends
 instructing others as to how to cook, fasten clothing, bath the baby, etc
 look at books and retell stories about other families and their lives
 make shopping lists
 read magazines and newspapers
 make telephone calls
 write birthday invitations.

Problem-solving, reasoning and numeracy:
 match plates with knives and forks
 weigh pasta for pretend cooking, introducing mathematical language
 rearrange the furniture, measuring with non-standard measures
 use a timer for pretend cooking
 divide a pizza between the family members
 consider vocabulary such as 'full' and 'empty' and 'hot' and 'cold'

Personal, social and emotional:
 care for a baby
 learn to take turns and share
 role play 'having a friend to stay' or 'giving the baby medicine'
 explore the emotions of a 'strict parent' or a 'naughty child'
 learn to lead the play and follow another's lead

This list is by no means complete and can be continued to explore the learning opportunities in other areas of the curriculum such as physical development and spiritual and creative development. The aim of such an exercise is to suggest that, provided the area is well resourced and that plenty of time, space and adult support is afforded to it, it is rich in its ability to challenge all children in all areas of both their development and the curriculum. Parents should not be too concerned, then, if this is where their children choose to spend a large proportion of their time.

This list of learning potential applies to the most basic of role-play areas, that of domestic home play. It is always appropriate to incorporate an area such as this in the setting, not only because it offers such a variety of learning options but also because it is familiar to all children, who can connect with it at a range of learning levels and feel confident playing in a place in which they belong. Other role-play situations, such as the "River Tours" above, or perhaps a garage repair workshop, will suggest different knowledge and new understandings that can be explored and practiced in the process of intellectual and cognitive development.

Learning new knowledge

Margaret Meek writes that 'The most strenuous period of imaginative activity is that time in childhood when we play with the boundaries of our view of the world: sense and nonsense, real and fictive, the actual and the possible, all within the cultural domain we inhabit'.[172] Here, she is suggesting that, as we found in the role play scenario of the boating expedition, imaginative learning is 'strenuous': it's definitely not an easy option. She goes on to explain that this is because children are at the 'boundaries', or the very edges of their understanding, which is never a comfortable place to be. Some of the new knowledge that children are wrestling with during this type of play is difficult cognitive material: for example, 'What is real and what is fiction?', and 'What are the rules of engagement with each type of activity?' We can observe children trying to work out the boundaries that apply to both reality and fiction as they often assure adults and each other 'We're only playing' as they display outrageous behaviour that they justify as being within the rules of the game. It was Piaget who first emphasised that children create their own understandings of the world by their experiences of it and that, by projecting their ideas into an imaginary world, they can stretch their intellectual capabilities. Vygotsky considered that the complexity of the process involved in abstract thought; he suggested that the idea of 'What if?' made imagination the highest level of cognitive functioning. Taking this idea into the adult world, it is possible to reflect that no invention, no great piece of music or writing, no beautiful bridge or painting would ever be possible without the creator projecting his or her ideas into their own imaginative world of 'What if?' and wrestling with the possibilities. The process of the toddler 'feeding the baby' and the architect designing a new building are arguably the same, albeit at opposite ends of the continuum. We can picture this process by thinking of Bruner's Spiral Curriculum, which will be considered at some length later in this chapter. The toddler might be at the bottom, or earliest stage of the spiral with his imaginative skills just emerging, and the architect might be at the top. At whatever level of expertise, the individual creator is at, the 'actual' and the 'possible' live side by side in each creative mind.

This high level of imaginative functioning needs to be clearly separated from the process of reproducing other people's ideas that is often seen in settings. Perhaps springing from the erroneous idea that young children cannot have original ideas or perhaps, from a concern that staff do not have the understanding themselves to support children in the process of critical and imaginative thought, there are many settings where children are safe and compliant but not intellectually excited and challenged. Here will be seen resources that can have only one function, staff whose major priority is management and orderliness and where time is divided into small chunks. The environment, both the inside, and outside as well as the emotional environment, is often referred to as the 'third educator', the first being the parents and the second being the teacher. The environment that supports children's innovative thinking needs to be flexible, mainly child-initiated and to function through a curriculum that is open-ended so that children's ideas are nurtured and can flourish. Staff do not need to be 'super intelligent' to encourage and facilitate children's imagination, they need to provide a place where children are loved and their creations valued and to understand that, as the EYFS reminds us, 'every child is a competent learner from birth'. What children lack, is not competence, but experience, and that is just what the knowledgeable practitioner can provide.

The spiral curriculum

We considered this model of learning in Chapter 2. Bruner suggested that the idea of the spiral was helpful in supporting children to become increasingly proficient at the area of learning they are engaged in. As children have increasing opportunities to practice the thing they are learning about, they become more secure in their knowledge and can progress to more complex understandings. The implication for us as practitioners is that, for children to become more knowledgeable and more competent, the provision or activity has to be consistently available to them or progress cannot occur. If we think about the process of learning to ride a two-wheeled bike, it is necessary that the bike is available for constant practice because only then will the new rider get enough experience and thus confidence to keep practising and get more accomplished. The child who is learning about, for example, what it is like to be a garage mechanic, needs to be able to dress in the overalls, handle screwdrivers and pumps and learn some of the mechanical language that will describe faulty brakes, punctures and empty fuel tanks. Bruner's argument was that in order to become secure in this new knowledge, to truly become mechanics, children must have access to the play regularly, as every play session will advance their understanding and enable them to play in more complex and sophisticated ways. In this way, the child moves up the spiral towards the top and will be well placed to progress through Margaret Carr's 'learning stories' from 'finding something of interest here' towards 'taking responsibility' for the script of the game. (See Chapter 7 for a more detailed description of Margaret Carr's 'learning stories'.) The concepts associated with this learning become internalised as the child practices and becomes increasingly competent and eventually is entirely comfortable with seeing herself as a mechanic.

Symbolism and representation

Central to the success of pretend play is the ability to use one thing to represent something else. Children who have particular learning needs often find this concept impossible and are not drawn easily to the role-play areas of the setting where reality has to be suspended.

Symbolism runs through our lives at many levels: it is in print, in mathematical symbols, in paintings and in drama. A part of the business of being human is the need to represent our experiences symbolically and it is argued that no other species on earth does this: it is one of the things that identifies us as human. At around 2 years of age, the toddler will begin to demonstrate that he has got a grasp of this fundamental concept by playing a game of pretending to pour tea and offering it to a parent. From this point on, a world of opportunities opens up to the child as the imagined world becomes accessible and all things become possible. Bruner wrote on this subject in his aptly-named book called 'Actual Minds, Possible Worlds'. He called it the 'narrative mode' and imagination.

Bruner suggested that there are two uses for the mind: one is rooted in realism and the other is the narrative function, which is rooted in storying. The realism function of the mind is the one we use to solve puzzles, test hypotheses and advance explanations. The narrative function is the one that leads to good stories, gripping drama, primitive myths and rituals, which we all use to make meaning of our lived and imagined experiences.

Aiden Chambers believes that it is 'in literature that we find the best expression of the human imagination and the most useful means by which we come to grips with ideas about ourselves and what we are'.[173] Books and stories that recreate and mirror children's lives help them to confirm what they know and to experiment with what is new in the safe, yet exciting format of the story. Cognitively, stories, both retold and read, are powerful tools in the development of children's mental imagery. Once the image is securely embedded in the mind, it becomes part of the store of possibilities that a child can draw upon to turn an imagined idea into a creation. In role play, the store of imagined possibilities sees fulfilment in a replaying of well-known tales such as 'The Three Pigs' or, more creatively, in a variation which has been authored by the child. It must be remembered, though, that children cannot be creative with a tale unless and until they are thoroughly familiar with it, until it has been securely embedded in the mind. Only at this point does it join the store of ideas from which the imagination can construct new and creative meanings. The implication for this is that we must, when asked, tell and re-read the same stories over and over again because this is how children become familiar enough with them to use them for their own purposes. We all know children who can recite stories such as 'The Room on the Broom' almost by heart and be very certain, and indignant, when we make a change or leave something out. The reason for this is that they have a fundamental need to know every detail of the story so that they can begin, firstly to read the print that symbolically represents the story and, secondly, to use their knowledge to play with the story in their own creative ways.

Imitating experiences and transforming knowledge

To use their imagination to create a narrative, children need to imitate what they see and hear around them. To imitate is not to copy. Copying means to replicate exactly what has been seen or understood, but, in imitating an experience, children will rearrange it in different ways and use it to create something new. This is what is meant by the phrase 'transforming knowledge' . Children will absorb experiences and, within a sympathetic context, be able to transform them into original ideas. The EYFS Card 4.3 supports this by stating that 'When children have opportunities to play with ideas in different situations and with a variety of resources, they discover connections and come to new and better understandings and ways of doing things'.[174] The adult's role in supporting this complex cognitive process is, firstly, to arrange the learning resources so that they are flexible and can be used in a range of ways and, secondly, to be prepared to join the child as he struggles to make these new and original connections. Again, the EYFS Card 4.3 requires adults to be alongside the child and to engage in 'Sustained Shared Thinking'. The FPPE report[175] found that in the most effective settings and those where children showed the most significant cognitive gains, this joint thinking extended children's learning and helped them to understand more fully the process of thinking critically. This is sometimes known as meta-cognition or, thinking about thinking and involves children in beginning to plan their learning, to make reasoned decisions, to persist, to solve problem, to reflect on and to evaluate what they have learned.

The practitioner's question associated with children's cognitive and intellectual development in the role-play area is this: **'How do I know where children are in their learning and how can I move them on?'**.

Through dramatic role play children learn much new knowledge. They learn about how lives are lived in other families, other countries and other cultures and they can gain knowledge about experiences that they cannot, as yet, try out in the real world. They can, for example, drive trains, make cups of tea, survive a sinking boat or mend a broken motorbike. Practitioners have a substantial part to play in enabling these playful experiences to become as meaningful as possible. I well remember the frustration of a 3-year-old boy in my nursery who had asked me for a calculator to be a part of the props for the shop. When I gave him a toy one that I had bought the previous afternoon, he replied with understandable exasperation, '*But it doesn't work*'. I learned from my mistake that if we expect children to invest time and effort into their learning we cannot expect them to do it without the appropriate tools. We must give them props that are fit for purpose, though not necessarily expensive; we must also give them as much time and space as possible and proffer different types of support according to their needs.

To be able to learn effectively through role play, the child needs to develop the following:

- ideas
- a previous knowledge of the part to be played
- the ability to structure a story
- the ability to play cooperatively, to take turns and to share
- verbal skills for negotiating and proposing ideas
- empathy skills.

Staff will need to recognise how important these skills are and to plan ways of enabling children to develop them. Children require self-confidence and some maturity, especially when it comes to being both assertive and yet empathetic in the execution of a plot.

Staff may need to support individual children as they move towards 'working as part of a group, taking turns, sharing fairly, and understanding that there needs to be agreed values and codes of behaviour for groups of people, including adults and children, to work together'.[176]

The best way for adults to acquire information about the learning needs of their key children is good observation of the role-play area. As well as knowledge about things, people and places (as in knowledge and understanding of the world), staff will observe children learning new understandings about how to conduct relationships and about how to deepen their learning by planning it, evaluating it and reflecting on it. The sustained shared thinking that was considered earlier is at its most effective when it is at the point that the child can nearly achieve something. When a child can be seen to be almost able to take the next step in his learning, perhaps in developing a role-play plot or doing up the poppers on the Babygro, this is where the adult can most usefully intervene to offer assistance and suggestions. Lev Vygotsky called this the child's 'zone of proximal development' as it demonstrates the intention of the child: i.e. the thing that they would like to do next or are ready to do but cannot do without help. It is not an exact science, as it is not always possible to know what is going on in a child's mind. However, there are indicators that can be picked up by an observant key person and one of the tell-tale signals is concentration. A child who is concentrating indicates a thinking child and one who may be just at the point of being receptive to some help in achieving the next step. The value of the key person system is once again evident in this situation as it is the key person, with their in-depth knowledge of the child's level of development and of their interests and learning needs, who is most likely to be able to correctly interpret the body language that says '*I would like some help here*'.

The true value of role play in children's cognitive development is clearly recognised by the EYFS, where it wisely advises practitioners to 'value movement and dance as highly as drawing and writing'.[177] It is tempting in these times of valuing high academic achievement, to place more emphasis on reading, writing and number by placing adult support with these activities and by assessing them more assiduously. The experienced practitioners, however, will recognise that early years education is not an 'either/or' situation but what might be called an 'as well as' situation. While engaged in being the mechanic, the mother or the oarsman, the deeply involved player will be learning about the skills of life that have been discussed in this chapter. They will be learning about themselves as people, how to manage their relationships with others and about other places, lives and events.

They will also be learning about speaking and listening, about writing lists and notices and about reading as they turn the pages of stories linked to their play. They will be learning about counting, passengers on the boat and fares for the journey, as well as how it feels to mend cars, how to turn a spanner and consult a mechanic's manual. What is even more useful from the practitioners' point of view is that these children, deeply involved as they are in their play, will be enjoying their learning and thus learning to a much higher level as they have chosen to spend time in this play and their strenuous efforts show them to be '*working hard*'! While perhaps questioning the EYFS statement,

Principles into Practice card, that all areas of the curriculum (as they appear in the document) are of equal importance in young children's learning, there can be no question, as stated on Card 1.1, that *'each area of their development, physical, cognitive, linguistic, spiritual, social and emotional is equally important'*. The holistic nature of imaginative role play enables stress-free but high-level learning to take place. Practitioners will recognise this play as a high function because when they carefully observe this play they will see children showing the indicators of Ferre Leaver's scale of involvement and they will be able to record a high level of learning for their records. It is in recognition of this fact that the *EYFS Profile Handbook* requires a high proportion of assessment to take place when children are engaged in what it calls 'self-initiated activities'.

Social and language development

For the purposes of this book, children's social and language development have been considered together. Although imaginative play does occur when a child is alone, particularly when the child is just beginning to recognise the potential that his ideas have, the more confident and experienced the player becomes, the more likely he is to want to share his ideas and join with a friend in a cooperative imaginative venture. In the same way that we, as adults, love to share a good film we have seen or a great book that we have read, children will have a strong desire to communicate ideas for role play that have been germinating and forming in their minds. Here, we see the need for positive social skills, or pro-social behaviour as it is often called, alongside good spoken language skills, as the experienced player tries to convey enthusiasm and allocate roles in the play that has been devised. A combination of empathy and assertiveness can be observed as a player persuades a friend to accept the part of the little pig when, what is really desired, is the role of the big bad wolf. This can develop into a battle of titanic proportions! The successful child is usually the one who possesses the 'super skills' of learning that we considered in Chapter 1: those skills of motivation, social skills and confidence give children the security and the necessary impetus to know, with almost guaranteed certainty, that they will get their way if they persist. The usual problem is that the developmental attribute of empathy, an equally important social skill, does not always develop at quite the same pace as that of assertiveness, and sometimes an adult will need to intervene to protect a reluctant recruit!

Language for role play

The ability to understand and to use symbolism is crucial for the role player. Spoken language is used as a symbol to represent the actions being played out. The player may have a range of roles in the drama, such as the lead role, a member of the supporting cast, the director, the creator or the audience. The language requirements are different for each, from the directive, perhaps the consultative, to the reflective and appreciative. Adults have a vital role in modelling these types of language, often in their role as the audience. They can offer the words needed to complete a dramatic story, recognising that in this form of play children will need the language to describe emotions as well as facts. One of the values of a group activity such as this, for new or inexperienced players, is that by being able to watch and then to imitate more experienced players, they can develop their own skills and ideas. Exposure to the use of symbols, both linguistic and props, such as a stick to represent a wand, gives younger players the knowledge of what the possibilities are and gives them the confidence to begin to experiment with imaginative play themselves. It is for this reason that well-known stories work so well in the role-play area. The sequence and therefore the predictability of a tale such as *Cinderella* or *Jack and the Beanstalk* gives all players the certainty of *'What happens next'* and a familiarity with the story also gives a confidence in the use of the language needed to carry the story forward. All the players, and usually the audience, can join in with 'Fee, Fi Fo Fum, I smell the blood of an Englishman' or 'I'll huff and I'll puff and I'll blow your house down' and gain a feeling of belonging to and a solidarity with the action. This type of play also helps children to understand the structure of a story – that it needs a beginning, some action in the middle and an ending. This is a basic pattern, that when internalised, will provide a template which they can use as a secure base from which to devise scenarios of their own design throughout their life.

The practitioner's question, which relates to the area of social and language development in the role-play area, is **'How should we all act towards each other?'**
It may be remembered that, in the Introduction, the comment was made that, although this book is primarily about how children feel and act towards each other in the setting, feelings and actions will have implications for how the adults feel and act towards each other too. The adults need to feel confident at entering children's role play both as a player, if invited, and as a facilitator, and this delicate intervention may need modelling by the lead practitioner as many new staff do not feel confident in this role or believe that it is an inappropriate one for them to adopt. Indeed, there is a fine line between adding a learning dimension to the role play and disrupting it altogether. This is written by one who has found herself sitting alone drinking pretend tea from a plastic cup as all the original players suddenly found the need to be somewhere else! The decision has to be made as to whether going in to join play is interaction or interference. Research tells us that adults are often needed to move children's play on so that rich learning can take place, but it is much easier said than done and only experience and a genuine respect for children's play can guide a practitioner as to when the appropriate moment is to join in. A major factor in getting the balance right between interaction and standing back is the nature of the relationships within the setting. If children have trust in the adults and if the adults have key children whom they know intimately and with whom they have a close emotional relationship, it is less likely that children will see adults as a threat to their play. If adults feel emotionally safe to take a part in the plot – in other words, they do not mind wearing a big hat or pretending to be giant – it is more likely that the play will benefit from their interaction. There needs to be a culture in place which asserts that the children are the most important people in the setting and that adults are expected to

be alongside children as they learn, as well as observing and modelling language and actions. It may be that, as in the 'River Tours' role play described above, an adult needs to be in role to model the possibilities of how the area can be used at the outset. This is significantly different from joining in the play at the direction of a young child and it is this latter position that some practitioners find unsettling. However, if successfully achieved, it gives a message to the children that their dramatic play is valued and recognised as important and it gives to staff the knowledge that they are accepted and trusted by the children.

9 Writing, drawing and mark making

Writing is thinking that doesn't go away[178]

Often called 'graphics', this area of provision gives children the space and the tools to make marks, draw, write and design patterns, maps, lists and models. Like most of the other aspects of development that we have considered, not all writing, drawing and pattern making happens in the designated 'graphics' area, but will be scattered around the different areas of provision and used as and when it is needed. In this way, mark making becomes an integral part of the many things that children are doing every day in the setting, rather than being artificially confined to a specific time or place. The purpose of different types of mark making must be apparent to children. In other words, they must see a reason for writing or drawing or planning something and it must be for a reason of their making rather than a reason of the practitioner's making. This chapter suggests how to provide different types of writing and drawing activities, and discusses some associated issues – for example, the differences between handwriting and authorship. It will outline the stages through which children progress in their understanding of the purposes and processes of mark making. It will be seen that what they draw and write demonstrates their levels of cognitive, social and physical literary development. In effect, it will be suggested that children will need to learn about writing and also how to use writing in their everyday lives.

We need to be clear, at an early stage, what the component parts of writing are. What is it about and what is it for? The main purposes of writing can be thought of as follows:

- conveying information, instructions and directions
- expressing feelings
- ordering, clarifying, recording and reflecting on ideas, experiences and opinions
- giving and gaining aesthetic pleasure.

The following section describes one setting's reflections and subsequent actions in attempting to make their children playfully literate.

to Grandad Tahn
I wizh that you Lived nearer
to us LoveJacob

'Writing is thinking that doesn't go away'

The graphics area

In a small rural setting, practitioners had recently attended a training day on the subject of early literacy. During the day, a debate had centred on the necessity for children to enjoy their encounters with literacy in ways that would reduce the stress that some of them, and their families felt, at the length of time it took for young children to become competent writers and drawers. Back in the setting, the practitioners reflected on their day's training and agreed that the boys, in particular, seemed to find it almost impossible to grip pencils in the correct way and even to sit still long enough to write their names when asked to do so. This was despite the staff's emphasis on how important a skill this was and having devoted designated 'writing times' for the older children in the hopes of meeting the early learning goals in this area of the curriculum. Staff spent some time over the following few days observing children's mark making, and in particular their writing, and concluded that the problem centred around children's resistance to any adult suggestion that they should write or draw. Sometimes this was evidenced by children saying 'I can't' when asked to write and sometimes children just seemed to vanish when they anticipated that a writing or drawing activity was closing in on them. Some children had developed quite sophisticated avoidance strategies such as breaking the ends of their pencils, not finding a piece of paper to their liking, losing the eraser or needing to visit the toilet. Observations showed unwilling children, exasperated staff and little enjoyment or 'gaining and giving aesthetic pleasure' anywhere to be seen. Clearly, a rethink was necessary.

The lead practitioner decided to try a radical solution. She understood that children learn most effectively when they are active, interactive and independent and had seen the setting's children totally immersed in, and engaged with, their self-initiated learning. This type of learning was usually play and so she took the decision to thread writing, drawing, list making and map making through the children's play. Her team's anxieties about this plan centred around their view of literacy as too important an area of the curriculum to leave to 'chance' and that, although some children might well increase their writing and drawing skills while playing, many children might not, especially if they had free choice as to whether to pick up a pencil or not.

The team was eventually persuaded to try the new plan, mainly because it was clear to everyone that the current methods were not proving effective and causing distress for both children and adults. The lead practitioner explained that if there was a belief that 'in their play children learn at their highest level',[179] this should apply across the curriculum and not exclude putting pencil to paper. Why let children choose whether to partake in all other areas but try to insist on them writing? It was, she suggested, the 'top-down' pressure that was causing the resistance and she proposed a 'bottom-up' strategy to replace it. The plan, to be tried for a minimum of 8 weeks, was to support, to encourage, to praise and to extend children's mark-making skills and to find ways of making it enjoyable for everybody.

Staff found three rectangular tables that they arranged in a 'U' formation. Inside the 'U' shape they placed five chairs. This shape encouraged children to enter the inside of the 'office', thus committing themselves to spending some time there and concentrating on and persisting in their efforts. There was some open shelving on which was placed a selection of different types of paper, some envelopes, some postcards and a variety of diaries, calendars and some printed forms from a local firm who had just changed their email address. A class list was added and an address book. A notice board, made from ceiling tiles, gave children somewhere to pin up their writings and drawings and pride of place went to a homemade alphabet which was attached to the walls around the office area. The alphabet had been made in conjunction with the children, who had helped find as many children as possible with names beginning with 'A', 'B' and so on. These children had their photos taken, which were displayed alongside the initial letter of their name. Letters with no children's name, such as 'Q' and 'Z' had children considering alternatives, and eventually a queen and a zebra were drawn and attached to the relevant letters. Lower case letters were placed alongside their capital counterparts. This alphabet, which had become a frieze of children in the setting, was itself the centre of much conversation and it was this project that kick-started a genuine interest in letters in the setting's children and brought them enthusiastically to the graphics area. The children were also provided with a hole punch, paper clips, a stapler, erasers, a calculator, a ruler, a date stamp, a pencil sharpener, sharp pencils, crayons, felt pens, a ruler and a clipboard. There were some two and three page books already made up for them to write in, a desk tidy, a letter rack and some old stamps that could be stuck onto completed letters with Pritt stick. Staff taught the children how to use the equipment and modelled processes such as writing books and postcards, filling in forms and list making.

The next part of the process, now that the materials for mark making were in place, was to ensure that children had real reasons to write and draw. Pads of paper, pencils and Post-it notes, similar to the ones staff used for observations, were placed in the role-play areas both inside and out. Staff had noticed that, when mark making did happen, it was often outside with chalks and with water and brushes. They concluded that the atmosphere felt less pressured, as water washed marks away, making them less permanent, and thus offering more opportunities for children to try things out and make it all go away with less stress involved than there was in putting pencil to paper. Outside writing and drawing was now encouraged, with measurements taken of how tall the sunflowers had grown in a week and notices saying 'please leave' attached to the outside constructions that were awaiting completion. A 'spider' had been created in the workshop area and children and staff constructed a web for her in one corner of the setting. The spider began to write letters to the children who sent her pictures and messages in return. As she replied to each of the letters and drawings she received, children became excited about receiving these letters and were eager to take part in the process. Staff put up environmental print such as picture labels on storage cupboards and a diagram of how the wooden bricks fitted into the Community Playthings chest. In these sorts of ways children became accustomed to using print every day at the setting when going about their normal activities. Staff noticed children beginning to ask, "How do you write...?" and showing staff their writing with pride. 'This says....', children would helpfully explain, perfectly aware that their attempts to write were not accurate and needed interpretation, but no longer anxious that their efforts would be in any way unacceptable. Staff learned to praise and encourage, and after the 8-week period, they reflected on their progress. Observations were showing children eager to make maps, to plan their models on paper and to construct lists about what was needed in the garden trail area. The younger children and those with special learning difficulties were observed playing with the drawing and writing tools, becoming familiar with how writing looked and finding out what a stamp was for. They, too, were absorbing the literacy culture almost by osmosis. Now that staff knew to value the play element of the literacy provision, they became less anxious that children were not formally tracing letter shapes but were surprised to notice that children now seemed to enjoy playing with the letters of their name and to copy the notices that staff had displayed around the room. Parents backed up these observations by saying that, at home, their children were commenting about written lists, and letters on the fridge door and enjoying letter games. One mother asked the setting what she needed to stock an office area, as this was what her son had asked for Christmas! What the staff had effectively done was to change the nature of the learning from adult-directed to child-initiated and the children's engagement was now obvious.

When asked by the lead practitioner if anyone wanted to return to the formal way of working with literacy, no-one did. This was partly because, as well as the lack of stress and children's clear enjoyment, staff had noticed that one or two of the more competent writers were showing signs of achieving the early learning goal that had been the cause of such anxiety. A few children were 'writing their own names and other things such as labels and captions, and beginning to form simple sentences, sometimes using punctuation'.[180]

In Chapters 1–4 we considered the theory underpinning children's emotional, physical, social and cognitive development. In this chapter we will take those aspects of development in turn and think about how they can be catered for in the writing and drawing area of the setting. We will also consider the associated practitioner questions.

Children's emotional and behavioural development

It was stated in Chapter 1 that it is the 'twin strands of security and confidence that give children the motivation to communicate experiences that are meaningful to them'. Children's earliest communication is through body language and gesture and it is at this stage that they learn from experience whether their efforts at communication are responded to by those adults whom they depend on for their security. Once that security is in place, they will develop the confidence to share their thoughts and ideas in spoken language with those important people who they know will listen. This process is lengthy; and takes much of the first 2 years of their life before they have the understanding and the desire to communicate in other ways than by gesture and talking. At around this time, children become familiar with pictures, in books, in photographs and in the environment. These pictures are a form of 'representation': i.e. they represent real people and things that children see around them every day. Parents and key people who offer children photos of family, friends, toys and pets are helping the young child to recognise that what is important to them can be represented in this way. This representation can be in other ways, such as role play, singing and art. Children's interest in and ability to draw pictures of, for example, 'mummy' or 'feeding the ducks with granny', stems from their view of themselves as, firstly, competent enough to attempt the task and, secondly, well-loved enough to see their efforts rewarded with praise and love.

Self-esteem

As we saw in the extract above, children's attitudes and behaviour around the activities of drawing and writing will speak volumes about their levels of self-belief and self-confidence. Young children will not understand that they are being asked to achieve the developmentally unachievable by correctly gripping a pencil and forming letters in a specific way, often to ease the transition to a cursive script later on. Developmentally, these goals are inappropriate, not only cognitively, in that children do not understand why they are being asked to attempt this task, but physically, as their muscles are not sufficiently formed to enable them to have the necessary strength and control. Inevitably, failure follows and, as we saw in Chapter 1, children will struggle if, for example, they are expected to attempt inappropriate challenges. Self-esteem, then, is seen to be a key feature in the challenging business of representing one's feelings and experiences on paper, and play is the process through which self-esteem can be retained and by which children can be encouraged to experiment or 'have a go' without any failure attached and with the necessity for an end-product. Children are recognised in the EYFS document as being 'skilful communicators'[181] (Card 1.1) and this starting point is valuable in focusing practitioners' attention on encouraging and supporting children to express their thoughts and feelings. Again, the EYFS states how this can be achieved by reminding practitioners that they need to 'Recognise that babies' and children's attitudes to learning are influenced by feedback from others'.

The story below is well-known in early years circles but is worth reprinting here as an example of a cautionary tale. It emphasises how vulnerable a child's self-belief is and how easily it, and the associated creativity, can be extinguished by adults who work within a culture of certainties and right and wrong answers with an end-product orientation. It reflects a recent worrying visit made to a Key Stage 1 classroom where the class teacher said that her children were competent writers but could never think of anything to write about.

The Red Flower

Justin was a little boy who loved to draw.

One day his teacher told the class they were going to draw a picture. Justin was very excited.

He thought of all the wonderful things he could draw: a dinosaur, a ship on the ocean, or even his friend, Chris.

The teacher said, 'We're going to draw a flower.'

Justin was disappointed. He thought for a moment and began to dream of the beautiful flower he could draw. Maybe he would draw a blue daisy or even a red dandelion.

The teacher said, 'This is how you draw a flower. First, you make a yellowcircle in the middle. Then, you add six red ovals around the circle. Finally, you draw one straight line down for the stem and add a green leaf on the side.'

Justin felt disappointed, but he did as he was told.

Six months later, Justin moved across town and began at a new school. Justin's new teacher was interesting. She wore long flowing dresses and large gold hoop earrings. One day after lunch, the teacher announced, 'Today we're going to draw a picture.'

Justin waited patiently for instructions. The teacher walked over to his desk and asked, 'What's the matter, Justin? All the other children are drawing.'

Justin said, 'But I don't know what to draw.'

The teacher patted Justin on the back. 'Draw whatever you like, Justin. The sky is the limit. Use your imagination.'

Justin took out a piece of paper and his crayons. First, he made a yellow circle in the middle. Then, he added six red ovals around the circle. Finally, he drew one green line straight down for a stem and added a green leaf on the side.[182]

Agency

We saw, in Chapter 3, that agency has been defined as being more than freedom of choice. Choice suggests that children can choose between several given options, whereas agency is about developing an internal locus of control that drives children to create their own interpretations and invent original ways of doing things and expressing themselves. Children need a lot of confidence to move beyond ideas that are already in existence to try something new and untested. A substantial number of successful experiences of trying things out will be required to give a child the sense that his idea may be as valuable as somebody else's, particularly if that somebody else is an adult. This is why adults need to frame their ideas and intentions with great sensitivity, as a child will be easily persuaded to abandon theirs, as we saw in the 'The Red Flower' above. The major way to foster children's sense of agency is to ensure that there are real reasons to write, draw and design. A child who has built a complex garage from the wooden bricks will need little encouragement to place a 'please leave' label attached to his creation if he knows with certainty that the notice will protect his building from demolition long enough for him to show his granny when she collects him at the end of the day. Interestingly, the legibility of the letters is a secondary consideration. All children come to recognise that a piece of writing signals something of importance and reason and the context of the writing tells them that a notice attached to something that a child has been working on for a long time will say something along the lines of 'Please leave this alone'. The actual words never have to be read and the children have gathered that if something is really important, it needs to be written down. Without being able to read the notice, or even needing to, children will be most likely to obey its message.

The impetus of most children's early writing is about giving information or collecting data. Children who have had much experience of mark making with a range of tools and have sufficiently developed small motor skills to be able to form letters will begin to want to send invitations to their friends, make lists of names and fill in forms with ticks as they see adults do. Here their sense of agency can have full freedom as what they write or draw on their invitation is entirely their choice. Adults may well help in the scribing process, but the composition is in the gift of the child. Agency is thus a key feature of authorship. Children who are making up a story, writing an invitation or a postcard do need to observe certain writing conventions (such as the time and place of the party or who the postcard is from) but the bulk of the content is for them alone to decide and provides a genuine opportunity for the children to express themselves as they wish in representing their experiences or sending messages of their own devising.

Positive dispositions

Opportunities for children to write and draw are a part of every early years setting but it is those practitioners who believe that success will be more likely to result from playful experiences who will see children joining the provision eagerly and with confidence. It is because writing, in particular, is such a complex process that it must be provided in non-threatening ways. Ongoing provision that is always available for children to visit, leave and revisit gives them much more confidence than writing activities where staff are always present and are attempting to teach letter formation with, as far as the children can determine, no obvious reason. A positive disposition is a feeling that children have when they themselves want to do something and it is wise practitioners who harness this feeling of motivation. Children who want to record how far they have jumped or how tall their runner bean has grown in a week are those children who will more willingly put pencil to paper and who are open to encouragement by staff to tweak their writing to become rather more accurate. Just as babbling is an early form of talking and crawling is an early form of walking, mark making is an early form of writing and drawing and must be recognised as such. Just as babbling and crawling are rewarded with praise and encouragement, so too must early written attempts be valued. In this way, children's positive dispositions will be confirmed and their written output will increase and become ever closer to a readable script.

The practitioner's question here is **'How should children feel about their learning?'** Clearly the business of putting pencil to paper is one of the most complex skills that children ever have to master. Alongside understanding mathematical concepts, such as number, the writing aspect of literacy is amongst the hardest to understand, necessitating as it does not only familiarity with the idea of symbolism but also the knowledge about alphabet names, their associated sounds and their letter shapes. There is, therefore, plenty of scope for failure and the associated feeling of incompetence that children will experience if repeated failure is a part of their everyday encounter with writing and drawing. For this reason alone it is necessary to find ways to present these conceptual understandings and skills so that children can experience success and fulfilment and thus be encouraged to continue their literary journey. Positive feelings of success and enjoyment, then, are a key part of good literacy provision and should be offered as a normal part of the play-based provision. Children will usually attempt drawing before writing and will practice making marks before trying to represent anything. Staff must *not* be tempted to ask 'What is it?' when presented with an early drawing in their anxiety to have an end-product to show to a parent, because probably this early mark making is not a representation of anything; it is the child learning about how to grasp a crayon and how hard it needs to be pressed to make a mark. These early positive experiences are crucial in persuading a child that they should repeat them as they will receive more encouragement and the feelings of sensitive and responsive adult interest are enjoyable and confirming. Staff will see children making marks that are clearly 'drawing' with a letter shape beside the drawing that is clearly 'writing'. This is a notable achievement, as it is evidence that the child recognises the difference between writing and drawing. This type of progress needs recording as a significant achievement and, if shown to parents with this explanation, will help families to recognise the stages a child passes through on their way towards becoming a writer and a drawer.

Children who are encouraged to be an author will also experience positive feelings of creativity and agency. Although they will be unable to write their ideas for themselves, children do understand that important things are written down. It is therefore a recognition of the value of their ideas if practitioners offer to scribe children's ideas for them. Thus, authorship is separated from handwriting, as it is in the EYFS documents. It is handwriting that is hard for children to accomplish, as their ideas race well ahead of their ability to write them down. What adults are doing is providing the mechanical means of recording children's ideas, thus preserving the content and giving the message to children that their ideas are valuable. Children who experience this process will increasingly say to their key person 'Will you write this down?' and the key person, who knows the child's level of development well, will be in the best position to start suggesting that the task is shared and that the child perhaps adds his name and a few letters that she knows he can write. This is sometimes called the 'apprenticeship approach' and is not to be confused with 'doing it for the child'. It is in fact, a recognition of the child's level of development and an example of a skilled practitioner working with the child at exactly the point at which help is needed. Children receiving this kind of consistent support, sometimes known as 'scaffolding', will feel confident enough to risk taking further steps along the road to becoming a writer and begin to feel the satisfaction of knowing that they are competent and skilled at an activity that gives them agency as well as a variety of ways of expressing their thoughts, feelings and ideas.

Children's cognitive and intellectual development

Observing children with pencils, pens, brushes and crayons will give practitioners much valuable information about what children know about writing and drawing. Some children will have had little experience at home of using crayons, as parents are often worried about where they will be used and fear for their wallpaper and furnishings. This is a hindrance for the young child new to the setting because it is those children who have had consistent experience with pencils and crayons who will have come to realise their purpose and uses and will be more competent in their use. Practitioners will need to assess at what stage their key children are and make a range of provision available to accommodate the range of learning needs. The cognitive skills that children need to be able to write are these:

- competence and confidence in spoken language
- a wide vocabulary and an understanding of how to express themselves using speech

- a familiarity of patterns of written language through the frequent hearing and repeating of favourite rhymes and stories (such as 'once upon a time')
- a thorough acquaintance with alphabet names, sounds and letter shapes
- a clear understanding of what writing is and what it is for
- phonic knowledge and how this knowledge helps us to convert spoken words into written words (writing).

Learning new knowledge

There is a multitude of new knowledge associated with being able to write and draw. As a 5 years old once succinctly put it, *'Writing is easy, it's getting it to say something that's difficult'*. The major cognitive understanding that has to be in place is that marks on paper have meanings. This is the concept of symbolism, which means that one thing – in this case, drawings, lists, designs or writing – can be used in place of something else. Drawn marks may represent people and objects, whereas writing conveys ideas and records information. It is at this point that children need to understand the mechanics of using representation in ways that others will understand. At this point, drawing and writing differ. Writing uses a common representational code which everyone attempting to communicate by writing must master, whereas drawing can be an individual interpretation and therefore offers more flexibility to the young drawer. Creativity in drawing, as in painting and modelling, can be expressed by how the marks are applied to the paper, whereas with writing, the written code must always be adhered to and the creativity lies in the ways that the written ideas make pictures in the reader's mind. These concepts are slippery and take a long time to become securely understood and is the reason that learning to write and draw takes time.

Children will often learn to write through their drawing and will label their drawings to explain what is happening in their pictures. This way of linking drawing with writing has an honourable history, as comic writers and cartoonists have found this to be a format which holds people's interest and helps them to become enthusiastic readers. Sometimes, children who are interested in a transporting schema will enjoy using their knowledge about drawing not to draw imaginary scenes but to represent their journeys, perhaps to and from the setting or to the park or grandma's house. This is an advanced cognitive process as children need to be able to see their journey in their mind and then transpose it onto paper. This process is the same as the child who attempts to make a car out of cardboard boxes and Sellotape in the workshop. The child's mind needs to be able to constantly compare what is being thought about in his head to the reality that is appearing on the paper or in the workshop. Any adult who has tried mapping directions for a friend will know how difficult a process this is!

The most obvious new knowledge that the young writer needs is how to construct the letters that convey meaning. The writing child will probably know through their reading experiences that writing in English goes from left to right and from top to bottom of the page. Of course, there are many other scripts which are written in different ways and children from other cultural heritages will be more familiar with the writing they see in their homes. Practitioners need to be aware of these differences and ensure that there are dual textbooks and adults who will read stories in the home language of children attending the setting whose first language is not English. Other written scripts such as musical notation often interest children as they become aware that there are a range of written systems that convey meanings and ideas to anyone who can decipher them.

The stages of intellectual understanding that children often progress through are these:

1. what writing looks like and how it differs from drawing
2. writing's purposes and its function as symbolic representation
3. how letters and symbols are made
4. that people enjoy writing
5. that writing gives power and status to the writer
6. that it is a permanent way to keep ideas and information.[183]

(taken from Lindon, J. (2005) *Understanding Child Development, Linking Theory and Practice*. London: Hodder Arnold)
As they progress through these levels, the following milestones are often apparent:

1. Children will make marks or 'scribble'.
2. They will form isolated letters or numbers, often the initial letter of their name.
3. They will 'write' lists or pictures of what lists look like.
4. They will write their own name.
5. They will label pictures.
6. They will develop a gradual phonological awareness and begin to spell.[184]

At the beginning of this section there was a quote from a young child who said that what was difficult was getting writing to mean something. With all the symbolism, graphics and purposes of writing to unravel and start to understand, it must not be forgotten that the central purpose of written language is to communicate with those who see the map or drawing or read the writing. Practitioners need to concentrate on children's intentions and worry less about the process of putting pencil to paper. If children's intentions are supported and their positive disposition is maintained, they will have the motivation to persist in learning the new knowledge that they need to make them increasingly competent writers.

The practitioner's question associated with children's cognitive and intellectual development in the writing and drawing area is **'How do I know where children are in their learning and how can I move them on?'**
As with most areas of development and learning, listening to what children say, or communicate, and observing what they do is the most effective way of gaining evidence,

both of what they understand and also of their disposition towards literacy. Children who shy away when they see a writing activity in their vicinity are likely to be those who have experienced some failure or who have had little experience at using writing and drawing tools and have little understanding of the purposes of mark making. Observations will also tell practitioners which children are keen to put pencil to paper and need to ensure that their interest is maintained by providing for literacy in as many areas of the setting as possible. Mark making in the early years can be thought of consisting of several aspects that comprise designing, drawing and writing. Writing itself can fulfil several functions and can be for storytelling, list making, collecting and recording information, labelling and giving information, such as notices. One or other of these functions is likely to be appropriate in each area of the setting and sometimes staff will benefit from using a grid design with all the activity and provision areas listed down the left-hand side and all the mark-making opportunities filled in across the grid. For example, simple recipe cards can be on offer when children cook, note pads placed beside the telephones will encourage message-taking in the role-play area and sharp pencils at the paint table will enable children to sign their creative artwork. There are real reasons for all these activities that children will understand as they act as powerful motivators. Children will not try writing and drawing just because the adults seem to want them to but must be able to recognise that the reasons for writing are valid.

The specific teaching of letter formation is a skill that practitioners will usually tackle on a one-to-one basis. This is because every child will need individual help at a time specific to them and for a particular purpose. The child who is drawing a map to his friend's house will need, perhaps, to write '*up the hill*' and the child who is measuring her sunflower's height will need to write '*Wednesday the 8th, 20 cm*'. This sort of individual help is exactly what children need and it is not the sort of knowledge that can be taught as a group activity. Helping children individually at exactly the point at which they need it is sometimes called working at the child's 'zone of proximal development'. This phrase was used by Vygotsky to describe the specific point at which a child needs help to progress further in their learning, and without this help they are likely to give up as they are unable to progress alone. Jerome Bruner talked about 'scaffolding' children's learning, which is a powerful image as it accurately describes the surrounding and ongoing support that the young child receives from the key person or the knowledgeable friend. This support, targeted at just the right time, is enough to enable young learners to take the next step in their understanding and ability. Moving children's writing skills forward, then, consists of a balance between a whole-class culture of real reasons to put pencil to paper and individual support to enable it to happen.

Physical and motor development

In Chapter 3 we considered the links between children's mental and physical development. As children desire to move more quickly, throw and catch more accurately and draw and paint more representatively, their motivation will drive them to practice their motor skills to this end. Very young children will enjoy making marks in their spilled drink or yoghurt and, although this event does not always receive due praise from the adults who have to clear up the resulting mess, none the less this is one of the earliest types of mark making and is evidence of babies' intentional actions. Sally Goddard Blythe's work on the links between physical development and later writing skills reinforces the notion that it is those children who have enjoyed many opportunities to develop their gross motor skills of running, climbing and jumping who will be more skilled in the use of the fine motor skills they will need to write, to paint and to draw. We need then, as practitioners, to make very sure that we value the development of children's gross motor skills as highly as we value their writing and drawing skills. We must provide for the development of physical control, spatial awareness and dexterity for children as they will need all of these if they are to develop into successful writers.

Handwriting skills

For children to write with competence they need to have both secure gross and fine motor control and hand–eye coordination. To help develop these skills they need continuing experiences of:

- large-scale movement such as balancing, climbing and moving to music (physical control)
- manipulative movements such as using tools, cooking utensils and scissors (dexterity)
- small-scale movements such as threading and cutting (fine motor control).

Programmes such as 'Write Dance' have recognised the effectiveness of encouraging children to move to music as part of the preparation for writing by giving them opportunities to practice large, yet controlled, movements and to become aware of the spaces around them. The movements can then progressively become smaller as competence increases.

Practising letter shapes can take place in a range of ways: in the wet sand; outside with paintbrushes and water; and, eventually, on large sheets of paper. The key to success is to keep the activity enjoyable and to allow children to practice letter writing in ways other than on paper if they already feel that this leads to expectations that they cannot meet. Young children absorb atmospheres and expectations very easily and may well be anxious around pencils and paper but relaxed at writing in other ways that do not carry the same, perhaps unrealistic, expectations. Rhymes such as 'Incy Wincy Spider' and other finger games will help children to develop the muscles needed for pencil grip. Providing simple musical instruments gives children enjoyable reasons to practice finger movements, particularly those instruments that are plucked. Staff often show great concern about children who do not hold their pencil between the first two fingers and the thumb in the correct way for writing to flow easily. The child who grasps their pencil inside their fist is demonstrating an immature grip which cannot be changed in a hurry.

126

This is probably a child who has not had much experience at using fine motor skills and staff need to provide for this child at the stage that has been reached and not attempt to force actions that are impossible for them to achieve. This way lies failure and disaffection. For children who have plenty to say but find the business of recording it particularly hard, information technology may provide an alternative way to make their voice heard. Children are becoming familiar with information technology at an ever earlier age and, although there is no suggestion that it should be used instead of letter formation, it can bridge the gap by giving the child the satisfaction of knowing that their writing is being read, their meanings are being communicated and this lessens the frustration of not being physically able to get the letters down on paper. Information technology should be a useful tool not an end in itself, and never replace active, first-hand learning experiences.

'How can I ensure that resources are available for children to use actively and independently?'

The quality and availability of resources for writing and drawing are central to children's disposition to use them. Often, settings provide inadequate supplies of sharp pencils and crayons and unattractive, rather tired-looking pieces of paper to write on. No child will be inspired to write on a faded, curled-up piece of paper and if pencils are blunt or broken and, if no erasers are available, the task becomes almost impossible. Writing, as we have seen, is such a complex process, demanding all children's skill and knowledge, that if the equipment is tatty and uninviting the likelihood is that children will not be tempted to make the necessary struggle. Rather like asking a builder to build a house without providing any bricks, a child cannot write without the tools of the trade. If children are to write and draw independently, the resources need to be arranged so that they can manage their chosen task by themselves if at all possible. Young children can use erasers and pencil sharpeners if taught how to and will gain great pride in their independence. This also frees the adults from low-level managerial conversations along the lines of *'let me sharpen your pencil for you'* and enables them to talk to children about the content of their work instead, engaging in the 'sustained shared thinking' that will further the learning and deepen the understanding. There should be choices of paper, different shapes and colours, and envelopes and postcards. The range of resources helps children define their purpose and ask critical questions such as *'Am I drawing a picture or a map?'* *'Do I need a large piece of paper or do I need a small one that will fit in this envelope?'*. This planning process that the child then goes through before putting pencil to paper is evidence of a high level of thinking and the resulting mark making will be more purposeful and considered. Resources need to be stored at children's level so that they can help themselves. This self-organisation leads to the child feeling valued and respected; they are assumed to have made thoughtful decisions about what they are going to do – in other words, to have *planned* their activity – and they are assumed to be able to make suitable choices about what they need to accomplish their intention. Adults are on hand to support children in this progress towards independence but they may well be surprised at just how independent children can be in the self-management of what they do.

Children need to know where the resources are kept, that everything they need is within reach and they need to know what to do with finished work. If these systems are consistent and reinforced with new staff and new children, they become second nature to everyone in the setting and visitors will remark on how competently the children organise their own learning!

Mark making for the very young cannot be organised in quite the same way with the emphasis on independence of process, but toddlers can still make choices about where and how to draw. Large pieces of paper, often outside, can be made available for splatter painting and making paint marks with fingers or with feet. Here, it is the process rather than the end-product that is the learning, alongside the enjoyment that the young child feels in taking part in such an expressive activity alongside their key person, who will be enjoying the fun as well. Very young children can make marks in a range of ways, by printing with objects that are easy to grip, such as fruit cut in half or sponge shapes. They enjoy making marks in 'gloop', in dough and in wet sand and learn that they can leave a trace of themselves or an idea of theirs on their environment. An international early years conference held in Reggio Emilia in 2004 was called 'Traces of Identity' and part of its aim was to explore the basic need that everyone, even a very young child, has to make an impression on their world and to leave a trace of who they are as evidence of their value and individuality. Complex philosophical ideas sometimes have very small beginnings!

10 | Games, construction, puzzles and the small world

> Provide objects that can be handled safely, including small-world toys, construction sets, threading and posting toys, dolls' clothes and material for collage.[185]

Young children have been playing with blocks, games and puzzles of one sort or another for centuries. In 1560 Pieter Brueghel painted *Kinderspiele (Children's Games)*. In it children can be seen playing with wooden bricks. They are also mentioned by the Moravian educator Comenius in the seventeenth century. Froebel and Maria Montessori both used blocks which were intended to be used to teach specific aspects of the world and the child's place within it. Children have been playing games indoors and out, on carpets, and on hard outdoor surfaces for generations, their games shaped by the spaces and resources that are available to them. The Snail Race game, Hopscotch, Snakes and Ladders, Snap and Pelmanism are all commonly known games that rely on a mixture of chance and skill. These and others like them are seen in most early years settings and provide valuable opportunities for children to learn in several developmental areas such as their memory (cognitive and intellectual development), their dexterity (physical and motor development) and their ability to take turns and follow rules (social and language development).

One of the major strengths of construction toys, puzzles and games is that they provide a link between the setting and the child's home life. These resources are readily available in many homes and are therefore familiar to children coming to a new and perhaps unfamiliar environment. They help children to learn about the culture in which they are living, provide genuine reasons for companionship between adults and children and between children and their friends and are also a source of enjoyment tinged with a little competitive edge!

Puzzles, on the other hand, are a more solitary pursuit, a pastime that adults and children enjoy for the same reasons. They present a challenge, but the challenge is against oneself rather than against competitors; yet they hold the promise of great satisfaction when completed. They are often calming and, like a favourite story, can be revisited on many occasions, never failing to please. The 'small world', as it is often known, consists of all those table top or carpet toys that children know well and can use for a range of purposes, usually imaginative games, and they are often used in conjunction with small construction sets. Here, a wide range of equipment can be used in different ways to suit a child's individual requirements. It may be to provide a script for a complex play scenario or it may be experimental. As the EYFS reminds us 'Investigations may appear futile but children may be on the brink of an amazing discovery as they meticulously place more and more things on top of one another'[186]

The construction area

The construction area of a setting in a South London district was as spacious as staff could manage. The setting served an area with high-density housing and many children had little room in their homes, which were often flats, to spread out and use large areas of floor space for their constructions. The construction area was carpeted and next to the role-play area. This arrangement meant that children could move freely between the role-play and the construction, using both areas together in their games if necessary. As these games were, at times, vigorous, staff had decided to partition off a much smaller area for those children who required a calm building environment. There was also a need to provide for a range of children's needs and experiences. Those children with little prior knowledge of large block construction would need space to unpack and make piles of bricks and line them up while those who had been playing with bricks for some years would be using them in more sophisticated ways. To partition off the area, staff had used shelving and the big storage box that housed the large solid blocks to provide clear boundaries around the constructions. This was both to protect them from being knocked accidentally and to ensure that the building did not encroach on other activities nearby. Stored next to the large bricks, on the adjacent shelving, were the small-world toys: Play-people, small figures from different cultures, farm animals, wild animals, fish, dinosaurs, the train set, small cars, lorries, tractors, buses and bikes. Next to the small-world storage boxes was a large road map, a wooden garage and a doll's house with furniture. On the wall to one side of the construction area was a large piece of paper, attached to the wall with Blu-Tack and there was a pot of felt pens nearby. This was to encourage children to make graphic representations of their constructions, either before building began, as a design or plan, or afterwards as a record of what had been built in case it had to be packed away.

Negotiation was an integral part of the construction area as children were able to extend their building with the agreement of other children using nearby space. Often, the only way to find a large enough space to build in the grand style was to take the bricks outside and staff knew that they needed to enable children to use this resource flexibly so that they would not become frustrated in a cramped space. Unfortunately, children often wanted to take the bricks into the wet sand and make 'cement' to put between their bricks in the construction of castles, office blocks and swimming pools. This was because there was a large building site next to the setting and the children passed the cement mixer each time they came to the setting and were eager to copy what they were seeing on a regular basis. As this would cause damage to the expensive blocks, staff were in the process of combing the local charity shops to find a set of bricks that could become the 'outdoor bricks' and could be used more robustly!

Two tables were allocated for puzzles and games. These were also on the carpeted area of the setting and often children carried the puzzles and games onto the floor or into the book area where they felt more comfortable in an enclosed space. There was always a selection of puzzles offered, ranging from quite simple 15-piece ones to complex layered ones. Staff became aware at how competent some children were at complex puzzles. In fact, one member of staff remarked that if some of the layered puzzles remained unfinished when the children went home, the staff could struggle for a long while to complete them! Puzzles reflected the cultural heritage of the children attending the setting and had designs showing men in caring professions and women as engineers and doctors to emphasise a policy of equal opportunities. At a recent planning meeting one member of staff had suggested that children could make their own jigsaw puzzles. Some photos of children and their activities were laminated and children helped to design a simple pattern on the reverse which, when cut, would make a simple puzzle. The photos for cutting were stacked in a container designated for that purpose so that no confusion would arise as to which photos were available for cutting into puzzles! Puzzles were stored in zip-up plastic bags, which, although an expensive initial outlay, helped to keep the puzzle pieces from getting lost.

Children initially enjoyed games that they knew from home. Card games such as Snap, Lotto and Dominoes were easily recognisable and could be played with at a range of complexity. New games that they learned at the setting needed some watching and learning of rules. The setting would occasionally introduce a new game so that children always had the challenge of learning a new set of rules. Often, fierce debates would open up as children who had a grasp of how the game should be played attempted to explain the rules to a new player. More vigorous games such as Connect Four and marble runs would be stored on shelves that were accessible to children and collected by them if some suitable carpet space was free. Games would sometimes reflect the topic that the setting was concentrating on, such as the 'Insy Winsy Spider' game and the 'Snail Race' game in the summer months when much time was spent in the outside area. Usually, however, staff chose games and provided a selection of those games that were well-known as well as some new ones to stimulate children's curiosity and to provide a challenge.

In Chapters 1–4 we considered the theory underpinning children's emotional, physical, social and cognitive development. In this chapter we take those aspects of development in turn and think about how they can be catered for in the construction, games and puzzle area of the setting. We also consider the associated practitioner questions.

Children's emotional and behavioural development

The EYFS states that 'When children know that their feelings are accepted, they learn to express them, confident that adults will help them with how they are feeling'.[187]

Self-esteem

Many practitioners will have had the experience of sitting beside a child at the puzzle table and found that they were listening to things that the child needs to tell their key person. Often these are happy, chatty conversations but sometimes a child is sad, angry or confused. While the puzzle is being completed, children sometimes confide their feelings, knowing that they will be listened to and their feelings accepted. Sometimes a practitioner will make a suggestion, sometimes a note will be made later but, often, it is just a case of listening and agreeing that, yes, life is tough sometimes. For a new child the comfort of completing a well-known puzzle acts rather in the same way as making a cup of tea can do for an adult: it settles the mind and allows the mind to begin to focus on the challenge ahead! The familiarity, particularly of small-world toys, and the links that this type of play makes to children's lived lives, provides unique opportunities for them to replay situations that have significance for them. Children who have repeated hospital appointments will often seek out the small-world hospital sets and play through the experiences they have undergone time and time again. The small-world toys can echo themes that are being explored in other areas of the setting: for example, the full range of Playpeople sets such as the builders, spacemen, farm workers and drivers can be placed alongside the large construction so that children can make garages, farms, space rockets and new houses and explore the imaginary ideas contain therein.

It is important to recognise that the key to their successful use is how the construction sets are made available to children. There needs to be a consideration of what the rules are in terms of flexibility of use, and staff and children all need to be very clear as to what those rules are.For the best use to be made of large and small construction sets and for children to gain maximum satisfaction from playing with them, they need to be available for as long a period of uninterrupted time as possible. Jacqui Cousins, in her book 'Listening to Four Year Olds' quotes from a young child who used to enjoy playing with a small-world model making kit. Then he said 'I never play with it up here... I never... It takes too long to make all the little houses … . They got real little nails... I really like it .... .but when I build a house it takes a long time … . And then I got to break it... tidy up time'.[188] Observations of children faced with this situation would suggest that when children's train of concentration is interrupted in this way, a learning opportunity is lost as they will not revisit their construction to complete it. If this becomes a regular occurrence, children will lose the satisfaction that they gain from a completed model and the accompanying self-confidence that they feel of a job well done. They will become stressed because they are always racing against the clock and cannot devote all their energies into completing a satisfying piece of learning if they are constantly listening out for the impending directive 'tidy up time'. Children who are investing all of their knowledge, motivation and aptitudes into creating complex structures with deeply imaginative storylines need a lot of time 'to be' as well as time 'to do'.

The other requisite for best use of large and small construction is space. The amount of space allocated to constructions gives a strong message as to how important we, as practitioners, think the activity is. If it squashed into a dark corner and is untidy and gets little adult attention, children will recognise that the adults do not value this provision. They will be squashed too, and arguments will follow as too many children with too many different agendas try to play their own way in a tight space. Accidental toppling of big bricks will cause distress and so it is important to devise an area that is spacious and has room to expand on busy days. If well provisioned, this is an area of play that will engage most children and will often provide opportunities for deep-level learning for those children less drawn to overtly literary, scientific or mathematical activities. For this reason alone, it behoves staff to ensure that the learners who come often to play with the construction toys can learn at depth and in ways that are satisfying and valuable. As an area of possible learning it should be valued just as highly as the book area or the writing table.

Positive dispositions

We considered in Chapter 1 how children's curiosity can be aroused to motivate them to learn something new; the EYFS calls this 'New connections that help to transform our understanding'.[189] A young child looking at a set of Mobilo or the hollow bricks can see

'The possibilities for creating something entirely new'

inside their head what the possibilities are for creating something entirely new, sometimes called a 'creation'. The desire to set about this complex task with the necessary confidence is called a 'positive disposition'. For children to possess this 'can do' attitude to new learning they will need to know that someone who loves them and is interested in their learning process is close by to help when things get hard. A positive disposition to learning can be said to have its feet in security and confidence and its head in curiosity and new ideas. Children will not usually be short of ways to create new environments and exciting scenarios out of the construction sets and often staff will leave the blocks and sets of small-world toys in their storage boxes for children to access and use as they see fit. Sometimes, however, particularly if the play seems rather repetitive and 'stuck', adults will provide the occasional impetus by placing, perhaps, sheets in the large brick area for children to use as a cover to make a 'cave' or a rope and pulley can be fixed in place for children to use to lift and lower 'building equipment'. When the construction area is close to the role-play area, blocks can be taken into the house and used as beds and walls while pots and pans taken from the home area into the construction area can deepen the level of play here. Flexible use by both adults and children will enable the play to be of a higher level as the creative opportunities grow, and as children see their 'agency' or influence over the play grow they will be further motivated or 'disposed' to think ever more deeply about what they are learning about.

'How should children feel about themselves and their learning in the construction area?'

It is necessary to look, first, at what is on offer in terms of genuine learning opportunities and, secondly, how the resources are made available to children. If the equipment is fit for purpose – i.e. it is appropriate and plentiful and varied enough to spark children's curiosity – children will most probably feel motivated to use it to create different places to play and invent accompanying play scripts. If the resources are well stored and labelled and children can access them all easily and use them in different areas of the setting, they will most probably feel positive about engaging with them in the knowledge that they have a measure of control and some independence over their use. Children need to feel attracted to the resources themselves and then to the possibilities that they offer in order to exploit the potential of this learning area to the full. From the comfort of a well-known puzzle, to the excitement and challenge of a new game or a new area to create, these resources cater for the full range of children's needs. It is, indeed, possible to teach most of the Foundation Stage curriculum through this equipment if it is sensitively and responsively offered.

Children's cognitive and intellectual development

In this section the possibilities of learning new knowledge in the construction, games and puzzle area will be examined, as well as other aspects of children's cognitive development such as the encouragement of creativity, attitudes to learning and the role of the adult in observing and assessing children's learning.

Learning new knowledge

The new areas of knowledge most commonly associated with the large and small construction areas of the early years setting are probably those linked to mathematics, technology and the development of creative and imaginary thinking. The earliest experiences with large construction, which may be the resource less familiar to the new player, are concerned with the nature and properties of the bricks and planks and what can be done with them. In Chapter 7 we considered the levels of progression that children often pass through on their journey from 'watching and taking an interest' to 'taking responsibility' for their learning. With the large construction equipment, children will need to spend much time packing, unpacking, sorting, arranging, lining up building towers and knocking them down before they are ready to use the blocks creatively. Intellectually, blocks help children learn across the curriculum. Young children develop their vocabularies as they learn to describe sizes, shapes and positions. They can develop mathematical skills by grouping, adding and subtracting with blocks. Older children make early experiments with gravity, balance, and geometry. In her book *'Exploring Learning: Young Children and Blockplay'*, Pat Gura describes three years of observational research into young children's block play and asserts that, at a complex level of use, playing with blocks acts as a powerful means of non-verbal communication. In this in-depth study, aesthetics, the processes of science and problem-solving are all presented as part of the reality of block play.[190]

When considering the curriculum area of science and technology, the different types of playing with large construction equipment might be considered as follows:

- *Building*, with hollow and solid unit blocks, blocks of varying sizes, some square and some rectangular. Learning about the vertical and the horizontal, balance and strength.
- *Taking apart and putting together materials,* wooden or plastic 'take-apart' trucks and cars that snap or screw together, large interlocking blocks and boards, clip-on wheels and trailers, interlocking train tracks and connectors.
- *Filling and emptying* dump trucks, boxes, cartons, baskets, cans, buckets, picnic baskets, small blocks, small vehicles, people, animals, doll's house furniture, stones and shells.

Here, children will learn new knowledge about maths too. Counting, setting, classification, measuring and geometric shapes all abound in this area of provision. Children exploring mathematical and scientific schemas will be found regularly in this part of the setting as they experiment and become more proficient with vertical and lateral trajectories, enclosure, connection and transporting. One of the reasons that this area is so popular with young children is that construction materials have no 'right or wrong' answers. Each child can make of the bricks and planks what they will; a set of blocks provides an endless set of opportunities to arrange and rearrange the world to fit in with what the child is currently interested in learning. Discovering how to make a plank balance to make a see-saw or ramps slope to represent a car park, or how to construct a wall that won't fall down are powerful learning moments where the child is assimilating, mastering and internalising fundamental concepts.

In some way, the learning implicit in the completion of puzzles mirrors that of the block area. Although puzzles do have 'right and wrong answers', in that they can only be completed in one, prescribed, way, they do teach that small pieces of knowledge, once understood, can be fitted alongside the next piece to make a whole that is deeply satisfying. The gradual revelation of a complete picture which is built up from an initial muddle of seemingly unrelated fragments is as satisfying to the child as creating a new world from, say, a pile of bricks and some rainforest animals.

Creativity and thinking skills

New knowledge, then, in this area is largely mathematical and scientific but it is also creative and imaginative. Early learning with construction toys is likely to be about 'How does this brick fit here?' and perhaps even 'Will this plank bend or break?'. As children gradually begin to understand the properties of the wooden or plastic construction sets they are using, they will be gaining in competence in the concept of working in three dimensions. They will then begin to use the equipment for their own purposes, which are likely to be creative. Although some children, particularly those exploring a connecting schema, will construct train tracks and roads that travel the entire distance across the setting and often, resources allowing, into the outside area as well, most children will be drawn to creating individual environments for their imaginative play.

In Chapters 7 and 8 we considered in depth how imaginative play is defined by the resources available and the construction area is no different. Although 'things' are the practical and physical props that are provided for creative play, it is what the children imagine that they can do with the props that provide the ideas that will take them to new places and engage them in new experiences. On the very day that my 18-year-old daughter left Heathrow Airport on her 'gap' year to Australia, my nursery children were involved in a dramatic 'plane crash' game in the construction area! I endured with fortitude the ensuing hours as they repeatedly crashed their planes, retrieved the bodies and luggage and struggled to extinguish the resulting fires. There was no question that they were pretending; for the entire duration of the game they were deeply engaged in a real experience that involved all their cognitive, physical and emotional forces in an integrated and powerful representation of a cataclysmic event. We were all exhausted at the end of the session as I anxiously awaited the reassuring call from my travelling daughter!

Symbolic thought and representation

Sets of large and small construction and small-world toys are an ideal resource for embedding the concept of symbolism into children's minds. They come with no instructions and are there purely for children to use how *they* wish: this process is known as child-initiated learning. They provide an excellent opportunity for children to practice the concept of representation by allowing them to find out, first, what the equipment can do, and then, what they can do with it. They will have already had experiences of making one thing stand for something else, such as a brick being used as a telephone, or a doll being a baby, and this area of play allows for this understanding to move forward in both scale and complexity. Here, children can use groups of families, animals and people to symbolise rainforest scenes, train stations, space adventures and the like, moving towards ever more involved scenarios. The creativity lies in the storylines that accompany the placing of the equipment. How will the players physically construct the resources to replicate a raging sea or a dark mysterious cave in which hides a fierce bear? It is in this type of play that children are learning 'at their highest level'[191] and when observing what they do in free-flow it is hard to disagree.

The practitioner's question here is: **'How do I know where children are in their learning and how can I move them on?'**
Staff sometimes feel uncomfortable joining in children's play in the construction area as it is so clearly an area for child-initiated play and adults are rightly wary of cramping the style of children who are creating new worlds of their own imagining. However, being around the bricks is a helpful place for adults to be as they can monitor the levels of concentration, problem-solving and inventiveness while also checking that the play is inclusive of all those children who wish to be included. Some children find it very hard to become part of a play scenario as they lack the skills and sometimes the language to gain admittance. Here, adults have a vital role to play as they support the enthusiastic newcomer by modelling phrases such as *'Can I be the tractor driver?'* or simply *'I want to play'*. By giving children the words they need to become a part of the game, they have not only helped children to feel better about themselves and raised their self-esteem but also given them the tools to use on future occasions when they wish to gain admittance. By being close by, adults can observe how much the children are learning in various areas of the curriculum. Staff are usually surprised at the amount of science and mathematical learning that takes place here and they will also notice some advanced spoken language skills as children, who are excited by their invented storylines, are motivated to dig deep for the expressive language they need to communicate with the other actors to tell them what they need to know and how to further the plot.
The adult role with games is a rather different one. Usually children will want an adult to play with, often because they have had a family member to share a game with at home and often because they know that there are specific rules attached to games and that they may need help with them.

A wise practitioner will gauge at what level of understanding a child is and pitch their partnership at the developmental level the particular child has reached rather than suffer the frustration of trying to insist on rules that a child does not understand. Anyone who has tried playing Snakes and Ladders with a child who does not understand the concept of 'counting on' will recognise this dilemma! Just as with any other aspect of learning, children need to play *with* the Snap cards, the dice, the lotto pieces or the dominoes at their own level before being expected to be able to play games with specific rules. Adults need to be sensitive and responsive to children at whatever level they are at so that they can feel satisfaction with their play; then they can be encouraged to move gradually nearer the designated purpose of the game as and when appropriate.

Physical and motor development

In Chapter 3 we considered what was described by Sally Goddard Blythe as the A,B,C of successful learning. In her work on children's physical development, she suggested that the cornerstones of successful learning can be thought of as *attention*, *balance* and *coordination*.[192] It is in the large and small construction areas that these particular skills can be seen being developed on a daily basis. Children are usually exuberant in their displays of physical prowess, often delighted to show how adept they are at running, clambering and jumping. With the bricks and small world however, a rather different set of physical skills is demanded. Children cannot be uncontrolled when trying to assemble a building in which they can hide. They will need to be able exercise great control over their physical abilities as they hold a plank steady until it is firmly balanced or as they ease the last brick into place in a high wall. It is here that the EYFS requirement for practitioners to help children 'Improve their skills of coordination, control, manipulation and movement' applies most sensibly as they learn the importance of hand–eye coordination and fine motor skills in the process of playing their games. As Janet Moyles states in *The Excellence of Play*, 'they acquire, refine and apply a range of skills which include: grasping, sliding, rotating, slotting, pulling, pushing, winding and stacking'.[193] This is particularly so in the playing of games and when using the small-world toys. Children will need to have developed the fine motor skills involved in placing, perhaps, the tiny lambs alongside their mother or the jigsaw pieces in exactly the correct positions to complete the picture. Small construction sets such as Polydron are helpful in giving children useful practice at using interlocking shapes to make both two-dimensional and three-dimensional shapes. Advanced fine motor skills are needed to join and rejoin these tiles and failure is a common feature at first. However, children do not seem daunted by the advanced skills needed and will usually persist until a complex shape is finally achieved. The great satisfaction experienced is worth all the struggle and the secret to children's persistence is that the resource is available on a regular basis and comes with no instructions and no end-product is expected. Children can join the shapes together as they choose and construct as simple or as complex a shape as they like, depending on what is developmentally appropriate.

So, 'How can I ensure that resources are available for children to use actively and independently?'

A key aspect to successful use of the construction, games and puzzle area is their storage and the setting's rules regarding their use. A sensible rule of thumb is that if the children can see the equipment, they should be free to access it. If staff wish to be selective and restrict children's access to a small range of choices, they need to lock away from viewing anything that they do not wish to be used. To enable children to make choices and have some autonomy over their learning, they should be able to choose between perhaps the Lego and the Playmobil. Once children have a choice, they can engage in critical thinking along the lines of "What do I want to play and which resource will best enable me to play my way?' or 'If I want to play at being a farmer, do I need the ambulances or the tractors?'. Although this may sound simplistic to us as adults, it is these straightforward choices that help children begin to make thoughtful selections. It helps them to think critically and to experience having some agency over what happens to them as their choices are respected. On the other hand, too many choices can overwhelm a child who may be new to selecting from a range of options. A chaotic environment, with the carpet area covered in a muddled heap of unrelated equipment, will not help children to engage in their play at a high level. They will be unable to concentrate and to persist with their storyline if they are tripping over train sets when they are thinking about constructing a cave for a dragon. This is where negotiation often comes in. Staff may have taken the sensible decision to limit the resources so that those that are available match the current interest of the children. Thus, if the children have been enjoying the story '*Thomas The Tank Engine*'[194] by the Reverend W. Awdry, there may well be train sets and a farm set ready to be played with in the construction area. This, however, should be only a staff suggestion and not a directive. Should the children arrive at the setting having walked around a building site where the cranes and diggers have just started work, staff should be flexible enough to agree to let children pack away the trains and animals and fetch the building site equipment, provided, of course, that other children agree. This, perhaps is the beginning of learning about how a democracy functions!

Children should be able to spread out their construction toys to enable them to fully exploit the potential of the resources. However, staff need to balance the needs of children in the areas adjacent to the construction with players eager to cover the entire setting with their layouts. Negotiation, again, is helpful here as staff make suggestions as to how generous they can be with space; perhaps another part of the setting might be made available or perhaps there are just too many large bricks for the small area allocated? Planning the amount of equipment to match the amount of space in which it is to be used is a basic organisational task which can have a huge impact on the success of an area. Finally, all these resources – the bricks, the games, the puzzles and the small-world toys – need regular overhauling for cleanliness and for usability. One does not have to be a child to experience the frustration of trying to complete a jigsaw which has a piece missing or to try playing with the marble run which has lost its marbles! As a rule of thumb, anything that has not been used, or played with, in the past 12 months should be disposed of. Regular housekeeping is a vital aspect of good early years practice and one which may be somewhat unrecognised as playing a significant part in enabling children to play and to learn in satisfying and productive ways.

Social and language development

The construction area, in particular, is a valuable asset in terms of providing children with opportunities to interact and to use spoken language to explain their imaginative plots to their fellow players. The concept of a genuinely joint project, one where the object of the construction is the same for all the players, is both cognitively complex and requires a high level of self-confidence and responsiveness on the part of the players. Often in early years settings when we see children playing alongside each other, each child has, in their mind, their individual intention. A large construction project, however, demands one child's intention to be accepted by all the players. The 'lead player' will have to get the project accepted by the others, will have to explain it clearly and consider how to react to suggestions that might alter the original concept. In one setting, a child was constructing a maze following a visit he had recently made to a local stately home which had a maze in the garden. The setting's long hollow bricks were being lined up in parallel lines to form the route that the maze would take and his intention was to make the route increasingly circular so that there would be a central end-point and a prize in the middle. It became clear that although the idea was clear in his head, he was unable to explain it to his friends, who were showing little tolerance towards his careful positioning of parallel rows of bricks progressing in a curved shape. His key person stepped in at an early stage and spent a while trying to interpret his intentions to his friends. On this occasion, he was left to complete his design alone as none of his friends had been to a maze and could not make sense of his idea. Although it was important for him to complete his maze, he did so in very quick time as he was a sociable child for whom the companionship of his friends was more important than making a solitary construction. Very soon, his friends returned, as his skills as a lead player were valued, and a more generally accessible construction of a bridge over the river where the big bad troll lived was soon in place. This game was understood by every participant and soon each child had been assigned a familiar role and a comfortingly swashbuckling adventure was underway with its predictably satisfying ending.

The practitioner's question here is **'How should we all act towards each other?**
A helpful response to this question might be that it is important to recognise that children learn about puzzles, games and constructing new worlds in just the same way that they learn about basic concepts or about how to read. That means that they need to explore, to try things out and to make mistakes and that this process needs to be understood and valued by staff. The uncompleted puzzle, the partly understood game and the muddle at

the end of a long time of seemingly purposeless construction is, in fact, every bit as useful a learning process as the end-product. This area does not produce the daily mess of spilled paint or glue that is often the result of exploration with painting and sticking, and there is not always anything much to show for all the effort that has clearly been expended in this area. Adults need to recognise that tidying and packing away is in itself a valuable part of the learning process and that children need to be as involved in it as the adults. This will result in less frustration as the often twice-daily task of clearing up comes around once more and a cheerful song to accompany the chore, such as 'This is the way we tidy the bricks, tidy the bricks, tidy the bricks' will lessen the tensions and encourage some rather more enthusiastic assistance. We should, in short, act responsively to each other as adults as well as to children to ensure that we value and recognise their small, daily achievements and share in the challenges and delights of making those achievements possible.

Section 3 Projects and cross-curricular learning

Planning for children's learning

This chapter is different from those proceeding it as it is a guide to putting the principles into practice: a 'how to do it' of child development. In each of the previous six chapters, an area of provision in the setting has been taken individually and examined to discover what developmental learning potential it has. This chapter considers how a child learns as a whole, or how a planned for topic will be experienced from the child's point of view. As we have already understood, children's development is interlinked and, when learning is presented in its most effective format, children will be developing in many areas of their development at the same time. This chapter takes some possible themes that are likely to interest and engage young children and explores how these themes can be planned and implemented to teach the EYFS curriculum content in ways that are developmentally appropriate. These themes provide opportunities for children to follow their own interests at a level that is appropriate for them as individuals through the playful ways in which they are presented. In planning themes which might appeal to children, the following aspects need careful consideration:

- the children's development
- the process of learning
- the curriculum content
- the learning environment.

All these aspects are of equal importance and practitioners need to recognise that children's developmental needs are not the same as the requirements of the curriculum. Right from the start of the planning process, the lead practitioner needs to consider the children as a whole group in order to think about their developmental needs and their interests before deciding on how the curriculum will be implemented. Here are some of the questions that might need answering:

- are the children from an inner city area and do they, therefore, need to be outside as much as possible?
- are they skilful communicators or does there need to be an emphasis on providing opportunities to talk to and listen to one another?

- what is the provision for those children in the setting with particular learning needs? Do they have equal access to the curriculum?

This type of thinking will then begin to inform the themes that are chosen by staff, which should, as well as engage the children, interest the adults too. It may seem unusual to consider children's developmental needs before considering how to complete the learning profile documents. However, it is a truism that if children are engaged in a playful way with a theme that is developmentally appropriate for them, their learning will be at a deeper level and will thus provide evidence which can be used to assess their learning levels. For example, children who are moving the furniture in the role-play area as part of a 'moving house' project will clearly be able to demonstrate that they can 'use mathematical ideas and methods to solve practical problems'.[195] Once the curriculum content has been threaded through the theme, the environment will need to be arranged to support the learning. This means that in the process of learning about 'moving house', for example, there would need to be flexibility, both inside the setting and outdoors, about where new homes of various kinds could be 'built'. Thus, the 'emotional environment'[196] of the staff must support children's often untidy attempts to dismantle and reassemble homes! The process of establishing a theme through which to teach in this holistic and cross-curricular way will be most successful if the children have been consulted about what interests them. It is entirely possible, and developmentally appropriate, to ask children what they would like to learn about and, with the help of large pieces of paper, to scribe what their interests are and how they could best be followed up. This gives children the very powerful message that their ideas are important to the adults and is empowering in giving children agency and motivation. Children who ask, for example, to learn about how spiders stick onto their webs, are going to be much more likely to remain engaged with this learning than if it was a topic imposed on them.

Themes will necessarily have an emphasis on one or more developmental areas as well as one or more curriculum area, which is entirely appropriate, as staff will consider this in their long-term planning and balance these in the next term's plans. A theme based on the setting's surroundings, for example, would contain a bias on knowledge and understanding of the world as children learn about their community and its history. The next theme could then be based on, perhaps, a scientific idea, providing opportunities for different types of knowledge and skills to be learned.

Once children have been consulted to some extent about the theme of their learning, staff will need to negotiate the theme's content to ensure that it will be broad and deep enough to provide learning at a range of levels to engage all the children. Some themes currently used in settings are not wide enough in scope to provide a compelling interest to either children or adults. I would suggest that 'People who help us' can be one such theme: It is narrow in focus and in practice explores surface issues only. This can result in shallow learning possibilities, often causing universal tedium.

The themes offered in this chapter will, I hope, be shown to have a substantial range and depth of possibilities and to offer children the flexibility to take the learning in the direction of their choice. The theoretical basis that underpins the implementation of these themes is that they are, essentially, frameworks on which children can hang their learning. They should not provide constraints within which adults or children feel confined but should be loosely implemented so that children can take ownership of the ideas that appeal to them. In this way children will be much more likely to persevere, gain satisfaction and take a genuine pride in what they learn and achieve. The themes considered here have all stood the test of time. They have been used and adapted to suit a range of settings and, because of their flexible design and deliberately wide focus, are capable of interesting and motivating both adults and children. One helpful way of judging whether a topic is well designed is its ability to give children positive attitudes to learning. If children can be seen to be engaged in high-level learning, practitioners will see the following attributes:

- perseverance
- independence
- pride and satisfaction on the theme's completion and success
- help being sought
- cooperation
- care of others, themselves and the equipment
- problem-solving
- coping with failure
- motivation
- enquiry and discovery.

It is important to recognise that this way of working provides fewer guaranteed end points or finished products. It is necessary for the adults in the setting to believe in an approach which Peter Moss calls the 'reflective professional practitioner' approach, as opposed to practitioners being a 'worker-as-technician'.[197] A major difference between a reflective professional practitioner and a worker-as-technician is that the former delights in a world of possibilities and uncertainties, whereas the latter requires the anxious pursuit of outcomes with narrow curriculum boundaries within which are 'fallacious certainties'.[198] This freer type of provision will provide assessment opportunities and show children operating at high levels of attainment but is not driven primarily by the need to meet outcome measures. Planning topics that will engage children need to be firmly based on, and they will draw from, the long-term goals and pedagogy of the setting. These reflect children's entitlements and rights of education and care. Nurseries within a school will have their long-term plans and the school development plan as a framework, and all settings will be working towards the early learning goals. Topic plans are sometimes called 'medium-term' plans, as they provide suggestions as to how the long-term aims and the curriculum can be taught in developmentally appropriate ways. They often cover a 4- or 6-week period. Short-term planning, which often takes place on a weekly basis, provides a detailed analysis of the activities, provision, resources, staffing and teaching strategies that will be employed to put the topic into action. Short-term planning will also consider how children's progress is to be observed and assessed.

The topic plans, then, are a brainstorming of ideas where the intended learning – or the concepts, skills and learning attitudes to be taught – are the starting point for the thinking.

'From here to there'

This topic was designed to be broad in scope to appeal to many children in different ways. It was also designed to support children who were working though a transporting schema and who were repeatedly playing games which involved moving equipment around the setting. As schematic play tends to be compulsive, it is usually sensible to provide for it and support it rather than try to constrain it and feel frustrated by the disruption it often causes. This topic was originally conceived with a science bias in a summer term where the high proportion of children interested in machines could use the outdoor space to its full advantage.

Having settled on the topic, which was felt by staff to accord well with the needs and interests of the children currently attending the setting, the children were consulted at small-group times and conversations were started about how things move from one place to another. The following words and phrases emerged from these conversations:

> I like it when I go to my Nan's
> My toys in the bath go fast when you wind them up
> I can run fast down the nursery hill
> Snails go very slowly
> I can dance round and round
> In the snow I can see where I went
> Wind makes kites go high

These became the starting points for staff to group ideas into strands and consider their accompanying learning possibilities, both developmental and curriculum. The following strands were identified as possibilities:

> *Messages: spoken, written, coded*
> *Journeys: How? Who? When? Where? What do we need?*
> *The way things move: direction, speed*
> *Types of movement: skipping, swimming, bouncing, hopping, climbing, etc.*
> *Making things move from A to B: electricity, clockwork, magnets, wind, water, gravity, levers and cogs*
> *Things that move: animals, people, toys, plants, machines, materials*
> *The effects of movement:*
>   *on food: whisking, grinding, mixing, rolling, grating*
>   *waves, sound, tracks, vibration, heat*

This is by no means an exhaustive list but it provided staff with some starting points. It was at this point that each strand was considered for the concepts, knowledge and attitudes that might reasonably be expected to be learned from it. Some accompanying language that would support the learning was also identified:

> *Making things move*: Pushing and pulling, tipping, water, wind, winding up, dropping, heat, electricity, magnets, force
>
> *Types of movement*: Swinging, climbing, rolling, spinning, turning, sliding, jumping, bouncing, hopping, skipping, swimming, diving, running, walking, flying, stretching, throwing, kicking, flowing, shaking, nodding, shivering, rubbing, fluttering, crawling, floating, slithering, shuffling
>
> *Effects of movement:* Tracks and trails, sound, heat, breeze, waves , ripples, transportation
>
> *Things that move:* Machines, wheels, transport, us, toys, kites, gliders, balls, animals, clouds, earth, moon, air, water, plants
>
> *Speed:* Starting, stopping, quick, slow, suddenly, slowing down, gently, speeding up
>
> *Direction:* Up, down, left, right, rising, falling, under, over, around, turning, rotating

The next part of the process was to agree a starting strand and then to trawl though the setting's resources to find what resources were available to support the learning and what would need to be added.

The theme of transport was decided as the first focus point and a garage role-play area was discussed with the children. Having discounted the possibility of mending buses, as not readily available, the children settled on the idea of mending the tricycles and wooden cars that were already in the outside area. A parent volunteered to make overalls for the mechanics and the first piece of the topic jigsaw was in place. Books and stories, rhymes and songs with a transport theme were found and it was during this process that it became clear there was very close link with another strand of the topic – that of journeys. These two aspects of the topic could run side by side as children made cognitive links between the garage repair shop and the journeys that they undertook by car (to see granny, go on holiday or to the supermarket) and those that they could do on their bike or scooter (to the park for a picnic, to post a letter, to and from nursery). There was in-depth discussion about the difference between different kinds of journeys and what they needed to take with them. Lists were made prior to packing bags and cases for holidays and discussions were had about which journey might require wellie boots and which journey might require stale bread. These kinds of conversations encouraged children's creative and critical thinking as they were helped to think deeply, both about knowledge and about ideas. It was the *ideas* contained within these topic strands, rather than the *knowledge*, that sparked some children's interest in creative representation of their learning. An example of this was when some children drew maps which showed how they travelled to and from the setting or to and from the park.

At this point in the planning process, staff needed to identify which curriculum areas would be taught during each activity and with each area of provision. The construction area, for example, would be set up with small hollow wooden bricks on which would be laid some level and some sloping planks. Toy cars and lorries would be run along the slopes and differences noted in the time it took to run the traffic down the sloping planks. Steeply sloping and gently sloping planks would be compared for speed. Journeys would be built with the small-world wheeled toys so that visits to the shops, the park and the train station could be constructed. Journeys such as this would include traffic lights, pedestrian crossings and speed limits, all familiar to children's everyday lives. The idea of creating journeys would then be transferred to the outside area where trails could be designed by the children and there would be more scope for magical journeys to imaginary places.

It is possible to see from these possibilities that an enabling environment for children's learning is being developed and that practitioners are 'planning an environment that is rich in signs, symbols, notices, numbers, words, rhymes, books, pictures and songs that take into account children's different interests, understandings, home backgrounds and culture'.[199] Specifically, in terms of meeting curriculum requirements, this strand of the topic offered children opportunities to 'find out about their environment, and talk about those features they like and dislike'.[200]

Opportunities for younger children to explore the way things move would need to be built into the provision, though this may well need to be separated from the bricks and planks. They would need objects and toys that move in different ways, to push and pull such as balls, push-along trolleys of bricks, wheeled toys, cars and machines. A small area would be set up outside where they could, perhaps on a carpet or under cover, experiment by moving across different surfaces and up and down slopes. This would give the youngest children valuable early experiences of getting 'from here to there'.

Examples of some of the curriculum learning that might reasonably be expected to come from these activities are as follows:

(8–20 months) 'have a strong exploratory impulse' – PSE

(40–60 months) 'interact with others, negotiate plans and activities and take turns in conversation' – CLL

(30–50 months) 'observe and use positional language' – PS, R &N.

(birth to 11 months) 'learn by observation about actions and their effects' – KUW.

(30 – 50 months) 'move freely with freedom and confidence in a range of ways, such as slithering, shuffling, rolling, crawling, walking, running, jumping, skipping, sliding and hopping'.

(16–26 months) 'Express themselves though physical action and sound. Explore by repeating patterns of play' – CD

The learning above, which can be expected to be observed as a result of making the bricks and outdoor 'trails' provision available, will not be the only learning that happens.

A rich learning environment will see unexpected learning as well, which is every bit as valuable as the learning that has been planned for. Once practitioners acknowledge that children are learning from everything that happens to them, wherever they are, there will be a recognition that much more, and possibly very different things, are being learned from the provision than had been expected. Particularly when children are playing, their learning is likely to be unpredictable because the ideas that the children are following are inside their heads and not inside the practitioners' heads. It is for this reason that assessment in the EYFS must be flexible and staff must be ready to see progress that is happening and that may well be outside the remit of the outcome measures. These measures, such as the ones above, give only a guide as to what might be learned and there will most probably be spontaneous or unexpected learning because the group of children playing with resources chose to use them in a particular way. For example, a group of children may have decided that their trail takes them to a desert island and that they need a ship, complete with flag and treasure, to successfully complete their journey. Although not part of the original topic plan, staff are wise to accommodate this into the theme, as it has motivated several children who are working hard to produce treasure, maps, picture clues and a suitable cave for hiding the ill-gotten gains!

The strand that emerges from the play about journeys sometimes leads fairly effortlessly to the need to send messages. The clues and maps to locate the treasure need instructions and directions and postcards begin to be sent from the children on the desert island to their friends still at home. Some children will want to send cards to their grandparents and this can be the cause of great excitement as replies arrive at the setting in the post. A trip to the local sorting office can be arranged, with the postman agreeing to make a visit to the nursery in uniform and with the post in the official sack. These types of real-life encounters provide the ideas that children need to make more creative connections and to deepen and broaden their play and learning.

Staff will need to monitor the progress of the theme on a weekly basis. It may be that many of the strands never see the light of the day as children are captivated by the ideas of making journeys, hiding treasure, running a garage and devising a road layout in the garden. If they are fully engaged (see the attributes of high-level learning above), the wise practitioners will let the topic run and add to the provision to ensure that there is a continuing richness while preserving the consistency that allows children to practice their skills and deepen their knowledge.

Alongside the 'journeys' and 'transport' ideas, cooking activities will show children different kinds of movement. There is a good opportunity here for adults to help children make those cognitive connections by suggesting that whisking, grating, mixing, cutting and rolling are also movements. An examination of toys will reveal that some of these can move: some powered by clockwork, some by battery and some by pushing. Races across the water tray by blowing boats from one end to the other can provide another way to learn about movement, as can homemade kites and experimenting with balloon power.

As a theme such as this has not prescriptive end point, practitioners will decide when the potential learning has run its course. They may well be surprised at, first, how excited children become as they engage with these ideas and, secondly, how interested families become in the topics. This is because they continue long enough for children to talk about them at home; parents may become interested, too, perhaps offering a few treasured moving toys for examination or to come and plant some sunflower or runner bean seeds and chart their growing progress. On one occasion some older siblings offered some exquisitely aged treasure maps!

A topic such as this needs to be ended gently, with children being made aware of an approaching conclusion. It can be a very disabling process if the child, who is looking forward to another day in the pirate's cave, discovers on arrival that today he is expected to be the baby bear in the Goldilocks story.

Just as the topic is introduced slowly and thoughtfully, including the children at every phase, its demise needs responsive and sensitive handling. Children who have been using the topic to explore a transporting schema may need particularly thoughtful treatment as they may feel significantly aggrieved if they are no longer able to take resources from one place to another while still needing to express their learning physically.

Sometimes there is a real dilemma in ending a much-loved topic as children do become attached to the characters who may have formed a part of an enduring and successful topic. Just as Father Christmas inhabits that half-world between 'real and not real' for young children, so too will the giant in Jack and the Beanstalk if he has been a central player in the learning for some weeks. Staff will need to reflect on and record the children's learning, both planned and unplanned, and balance what has been learned with potential learning from the next topic.

'The same but different'

This topic reflects the catchment area of a setting in a Midlands town. Children attending the setting come from a wide range of cultural backgrounds and many have English as an additional language. It was decided to think around a topic that would celebrate these differences but also emphasise the feeling that all children belonged equally to the setting and that there was much that everyone had in common. As well as being a topic that would enable children's perceptions about each other to be explored, it also offered opportunities for children to develop a range of their cognitive skills such as

classification	labelling	identification	matching	sequencing
observing	predicting	remembering	estimating	
counting	sorting	describing		

The topic was originally conceived as one that would centre around people; their culture, feelings, appearance and relationships and a large part of the work that followed its inception did certainly concentrate on this area. However, when the topic was aired in group times, the children's words and phrases, which the staff noted, showed that they had a far wider perspective than the adults.

This was a selection of their thoughts:

> I like pink milk but Jose always has chocolate milk and that makes it brown, but it all starts off the same
> I was different when I was a baby
> Susie wears pretty shoes because she's a girl
> This one's a big crayon but that one's short
> Then there's the Three Billy Goats where there's a middle one
> The small boxes go in the top shelf and the big ones go underneath
> Tom looks different because he's sad
> When I wore my cat suit Mummy didn't think it was me, but it was, really

These conversations, held over a few days, provided a rich fund of potential ideas from which the staff chose several initial strands. As with all these topics, the strands can be developed, altered or abandoned depending on whether they capture the children's imagination. These strands became the starting points:

> *People:* feelings, roles, appearance, culture, relationships, bodies.
> *Plants:* sowing seeds, leaves, ageing, flowers.
> *Music and sound:* pitch, rhythm, volume, speed, songs with repeating verses.
> *Games:* Pelmanism, memory games, sequencing games, spot the difference games.
> *Art:* printing, painting portraits, pattern making.
> *Making collections:* stones, shells, tiny things, blue things, soft things, wooden things, stories.
> *Materials:* wool becoming jumpers, cake mixture becoming buns, water becoming steam and ice, sand becoming wet, comparing properties of two objects such an apple and nuts.
> *Imagining:* changing appearance by dressing up and acting, using masks, disguises, face paints, wigs and hats.
> *The effect of time:* ageing in plants, people, old and new clothes, books, toys.

The language that accompanied this topic would, it was thought, primarily be concerned with mathematical and scientific terms than with the more affective area of feelings and appearances. Certainly, the cognitive skills listed above come with specific language which young children have had little cause to use with any accuracy. It was noted that, in the initial conversations, one child confidently used the word 'big' to describe the opposite of 'short', showing staff that some maths language work could usefully be done here by modelling the correct terminology. Another child, however, knew that there could be 'one in the middle' between long and short, or big and small, and all these children, by showing their interest, were demonstrating that they were at a point to be receptive to deepening their knowledge in this area. Staff therefore gathered lists of appropriate mathematical and scientific words to help the children articulate their learning with increasing accuracy.

Children who make collections of 'treasures' will be classifying them into groups. They may classify by number, shape, colour or size. It matters not how the classification is made: it is the skill that they are learning that is important. As children classify, practitioners can suggest accompanying language such as:

> That stone looks like the biggest. Can you put them in order from the smallest to the biggest?
> Are these leaves all the same green? This one looks darker to me and this one looks paler.

Words that describe scientific processes also further children's learning. Staff should give children the correct terms for processes such as freezing, melting, evaporating, spinning, whisking, rolling and beating. As well as giving children the correct words to describe processes, adults need to take the opportunity of developing children's memory skills that a topic like this gives. By asking children to describe the scientific processes they have seen, such as watching an object sinking to the bottom of the water tray when they had guessed that it would float, they are helped to recall and to reason. Memory is basic to effective learning as it enables children to accumulate knowledge and to learn from experience. They can then build on their accumulated knowledge and take that new knowledge back to the same experience with increased confidence and competence. This is an example of Bruner's spiral curriculum, which was described in detail in Chapter 2. Memory can also be developed through the games in this topic: skills of identification and labelling are offshoots of a child's developing memory.

The strand that seemed to attract the most support from both adults and children was that of 'People'. There would be different ways of thinking about and expressing ideas about themselves, their family and their friends. A starting point would be to provide mirrors in the painting area and to mix paint to a range of skin tones and hair colour with the children so that they could choose the colour that matched them most closely. This would focus children's minds on their appearance and their facial features and those of their friends. The role-play area could be set up so that children could change their appearance in different ways by dressing up and using masks: i.e. they could begin to imagine being someone else. Alongside these activities, group discussions about 'who we are' could lead to an exploration of how a child's family customs – such as clothes, gatherings, music, language and food – may vary from other children's familiar routines. Staff could provide photos of themselves as children and conversations could develop about growing up and growing older. To emphasise some aspects that all children have in common, as well as the differences, it was decided to try to find something that everyone in the setting enjoyed doing. After a lot of thought, it was agreed that everyone liked good stories and everyone enjoyed collecting things although, of course, there were many differing views as to which were the favourite stories and many variations of what they liked collecting! Making collections offered ideal opportunities for children to practice their cognitive skills such as sorting, classifying, estimating and counting. These two strands of stories and collections, it was felt, provided a good balance between the affective aspects, of learning, such as feelings, likes and dislikes, and the more intellectual aspects such as pattern making, collecting and developing memory skills.

Examples of some of the curriculum learning that might reasonably be expected to come from these activities are:

(40–60 months) 'have a developing respect for their own cultures and beliefs and those of other people' – PSE

(30–50 months) 'listen to others in one-to-one or small groups when conversation interests them' – CLL

(22–36 months) 'have some understanding of 1 and 2, especially when the number is important for them' – PS, R&N

(16–26 months) 'are interested in pushing and pulling things, and begin to build structures' – KNW

(Birth – 11 months) 'use movement and sensory exploration to link up their immediate environment' –PD

(40–60 months) 'express and communicate their ideas, thoughts and feelings by using a widening range of materials, suitable tools, imaginative and role play, movement, designing and making, and a variety of songs and musical instruments' – CD.

As with all topics, 'the same but different' needs to be implemented with flexibility and a clear intention on the part of the staff to follow children's interests. On one occasion that this topic was used, children wanted to combine the idea of things that they all enjoyed together with the idea of making a collection. The result was a class book of all their favourite rhymes and songs. Although it might be argued that there was little in the way of sorting, matching, counting or discriminating, as there was with most of the other collections that were assembled, it was, nonetheless, a task entered into with enormous enthusiasm and completed with great pride. Children chose and identified their favourite nursery rhyme or song and most made an illustration, sometimes with an attempt at writing a few of the words, to be pasted into a large book that staff placed in the book corner when it was full. Children could be seen showing their friends and family the page that they had made and then helping them to sing or say the rhyme. *The Nursery Song Book*, as it became known, was often used with musical instruments and taken into the role-play area to be shared with the dolls.

Some aspects of this topic took rather longer to make an impact. The differently shaped seeds that children planted in the garden seemed to take a very long time to germinate and some children had forgotten the sowing process by the time the seedlings appeared! However, the trip to the local garden centre to choose a selection of differently coloured bedding plants raised the enthusiasm levels once again and a heated debate was held as to how the plants should be arranged in the garden to best effect. A great deal of observing, sorting and reasoning went on before the flowerbed was planted up to everyone's satisfaction. An unexpected offshoot of the seed sowing and planting was the number of insects discovered amongst the plants in the garden. Ladybirds, caterpillars, millipedes and spiders were observed and identified and the occasional butterfly was spotted hovering on the buddleia tree. Although children were interested in the differences between the insects, it was the camouflage aspect of some of the insects that really captivated them. A reference book provided evidence that, indeed, camouflage was an integral part of the survival system of many insects and children began matching the green bugs to similarly coloured green leaves. The different leaves of the bushes and trees in the garden were enthusiastically collected, observed and sorted. Some children mixed a range of green-coloured paints to replicate the many variations of green that had been collected. Some made small, identically coloured insects in the workshop to hide behind their leaf. Although not planned as a strand of this particular topic, staff followed the children's interests and helped them to draw from their interests both in curriculum learning and developmental progress.

The area of the topic that proved the least successful in practice was the work planned on materials. It was probable that the cognitive leap of observing sheep's wool being spun into knitting yarn and water changing into ice, although interesting processes to observe in their own right, were links too tenuous for most of the children to make. Conversations by staff about water and ice being the same but looking different appeared to fall on deaf ears and eventually it was decided not to continue with these parts of the topic but to concentrate on the collections and the role play which had captured the children's imagination. Reflections and evaluations of planned work are vital as we know from our understanding of child development that children who are learning at a level appropriate for their level of understanding will gain from it, whereas learning which they cannot connect to will be unsuccessful in moving their understanding forward. It was decided, on reflection, that staff had been too assiduous in trying to get the children to make what were perhaps rather spurious connections to the topic's theme of 'the same but different' when the links were not strong enough to be apparent to the children. Even the most experienced practitioners make mistakes such as these and they provide valuable pointers for potential pitfalls that can be avoided in the future! The best teachers are not those who never make mistakes but are those who can evaluate their teaching as it is happening and can change track when they recognise that their chosen approach is unsuccessful.

The role-play aspect of this theme was, on the other hand, deemed by staff to have worked well. Children made immediate connections with the idea of being 'the same inside but looking different' and enjoyed making stick masks and wearing the wigs provided to become a different person or an animal. Some of the younger children found the masks worrying and so a home role-play area was provided separately. This enabled the less-confident children the security of being able to continue with the normal domestic play of changing of dolls' nappies, feeding them and putting them to bed.

The effect of time passing was an aspect of this work that particularly intrigued the older children. Time is a difficult concept for children to grasp because of their lack of experience of long-term changes. As young children's lives are lived in the here and now, the idea of waiting for changes to happen is confusing. Thus, the seeds were forgotten long before they germinated and changed into seedlings, buds and flowers. However, one idea that was successful was watching a poppy bud open into a flower and then die to become a seed pod, a process that took only a few days. The poppy was a good choice as it is a bold and colourful red flower and the change from bud to seed pod was dramatic and effective in teaching about the effects of time passing. Also popular were the photos of staff as children that they took to the setting. These were treated with almost universal disbelief as practitioners explained that the photos were of the same people but at a different time in their lives. A practitioner read the story *And Then There Were Giants* by Martin Waddell,[201] and for some children this book helped them to begin to understand the concept of change over time, although staff realised that many more experiences and much more discussion would be needed along the way before the concept became fully understood and internalised. An example of this sense of confusion was when a 4 years old in the setting was told by the practitioner that she would have 'wait a while'. She asked whether it would be 'a long while or a short while'. So words such as *'before', 'after', 'then', 'yesterday'* and *'tomorrow'* were built into the planning as the project progressed as there was seen to be a need to help children distinguish between what has happened and what has yet to happen.

Possibly the most valuable aspect of this topic was the opportunity it gave for children to explore the concept of number. Adults often assume that counting is a straightforward process, but those with an understanding of children's cognitive development will know that other concepts must be securely in place before counting can be successfully achieved. For a child to count five red sweets on a plate on which there are 30 multicoloured Smarties, they need to be able to do the following:

Match all the sweets to the known colour red.

Sort the sweets to separate out the red ones.

Order them in a logical way so that they can be counted.

Remember the number names, one to five.

Pair the ordered sweets with the number names, sometimes called one-to-one correspondence.

Know that the final number, five, describes the sum total of the red of sweets as well as naming the last sweet in the line. These are known as the ordinal and the cardinal sense of the number five.

This learning is complex and takes time. It is learning that has not reached the level of symbolic representation: i.e. there are no written figures in the above process, or sums or plus and minus symbols. The Foundation Stage is the place where children need to play constantly with collections of things – sorting, matching, pairing and ordering every day so that they become increasingly confident and competent at handling sets of objects and will, at a later date, enjoy the challenge of counting. Fully understanding the concept of counting is much more complex than understanding the concept of a 'ball', which we considered in Chapter 2. The ball is a relatively consistent concept – i.e. it is always round and it always rolls – whereas numbers are used in a variety of ways. Children will usually associate a number with the house in which they live, saying '*I live at number five*' and think of the number five as their house name. Or they will associate a number with their age, '*I am four*', and mean that 'being four' describes them in ways that are linked with height, which class they are in and, perhaps, what they wear. Neither of these uses of number has, for the child, an obvious link with counting objects. For more on young children becoming numerate, read Chapter 7 of Anning and Edwards' book , *Promoting Children's Learning from Birth to Five*.[202]

The topic drew to a natural close at the end of the summer when the flowers had blossomed, been admired, died and the seeds collected. Collections were dispersed and photographs returned to their owners. During the review and reflection process, staff felt that there had been 'something for everyone' in the ideas that had been explored and the record sheets provided ample evidence that a wide range of learning had taken place, both across the curriculum and across the range of developmental learning. Children had grown in confidence in mastering some complex concepts and had been seen to be engaged in high-level learning, as exemplified by the attributes observed, such as perseverance, independence, pride and motivation.

'Living in the jungle'

This topic comes with a big health warning! Wise practitioners know that all successful learning needs to link to children's experiences and this one, at first glance, did not. It was only used once and it was considered to be quite a risky venture. The reason that it was considered at all was because a member of the setting's staff had taken leave to visit her family in North Queensland, Australia, and was to be away for 8 weeks. As she had key children in the setting and was returning to them after her trip, it was decided that links with her should be maintained while she was away and she agreed to send the children postcards and photos from different places of her journey. When the parents were informed of the impending trip, they, and the children, began asking about the travel plans and it was clear that much interest had been generated. It was on this basis that the decision was taken to plan a topic around what the staff attempted to call 'the rain forest' but the children emphatically and consistently referred to as 'the jungle'. Eventually, the majority held sway and 'the jungle', swung into action.

The process was similar to the start of all such projects in that conversations were held with the children to find out what they knew about rain forests and what they would like to find out. Staff were initially cautious, believing, that as none of the children had visited a rain forest, their knowledge would be negligible and their interest easily lost. To everyone's astonishment, the children knew much more than had been anticipated. The setting was in a forces' catchment area and many parents had served in countries with a humid climate. Some amazing artefacts were loaned by families during the course of the following weeks and pride of place went to the mosquito net and the cobra skin. The latter inspired art, role play and dance. The families that had been stationed overseas had a range of experiences of living in different environments and loaned photographs of animals, birds and insects unknown in this country. The television had brought the rain forest into many children's lives and songs and stories such as *Down in the Jungle* and *Anansi the Spider* were already familiar to them. Some of the children had families in Bangladesh and in Jamaica whom they visited and so aspects of class discussions about tropical heat and different animals were familiar to them. Their experiences and knowledge provided a more secure basis for the project than had at first been expected.

The conversations with the children about the staff member, Mary, going to Australia aroused a lot of interest, mainly, it was thought, because the reality of her absence would not be felt until she was no longer coming to the setting each day. Christopher said he had a cousin in Australia who went to bed every day when Christopher got up and other children were eager to make suggestions as to which animals and birds might live there – toucans and crocodiles being firm favourites. The following was selection of phrases and words to come from group-time discussions about the possibility of creating a rain forest area in the setting:

> We'll need palm trees
> Sun cream and big hats
> Do crocodiles eat people?
> I'll bring some bananas for the monkeys
> I don't like big spiders
> Mum said I could bring in my coconut shell

From these conversations it became clear that many of the children had ideas about the rain forest, albeit somewhat non-specific! Much staff discussion took place as to where to draw the line between enthusiasm and accuracy and it was eventually decided to relinquish some aspects of reality in the interests of keeping children involved. Thus, when the rain forest interactive display was set up, toy giraffes rubbed shoulders with monkeys and elephants in ways that would not have impressed an environmentalist. The theoretical reasoning was that we were starting this project at the level at which most of the children were and that they would refine their ideas as they read more stories and became more experienced in the realities of life in the rain forest. For a few children this did happen, and a heated discussion about the lion 'being in the wrong place' did lead to its expulsion from the display. On the whole, though, a happy mix of forest, prairie and grassland wildlife cohabited for the 8 weeks of this project.

Several strands came from the initial discussions and some possible learning areas emerged:

> *Appearance of the rain forest*: the trees, the flowers, the forest floor, the forest canopy, the river, night and day, vines, humidity.

Wildlife: animals, birds, reptiles, insects.
Products: nuts, medicines, fruit, chocolate.
History and future: people, dinosaurs, development.
Sounds: animal and bird calls, rustling leaves.

The language that would accompany this topic was thought to be mainly about classifying and naming plants and animals but that there would also be scope for discussions about the environment and its protection. Books by Jeannie Baker, *Window* and *Where the Forest Meets the Sea*, published by Walker Books,[203] provided both staff and children with insights into both the nature of the Daintree National Park in Australia, where Mary had gone, and also the threat to its survival. As dramatic role play was seen to be a major aspect of learning about the rain forest, words to accompany this type of play would be encouraged. There would be much *'creeping through the jungle'*, *'hiding'* and rhythmic songs sung, reflecting the stock of rhyme and song books currently held in the setting, such as *'Ahhh!, Said the Stork'* by Gerald Rose,[204] *Have You Seen the Crocodile* by Colin West[205] and Julie Lacombe's *'Walking Through the Jungle'*.[206] These three books, in particular, were thought to be instrumental in bringing the project within the range of the youngest children in the setting who would enjoy the rhythms and surprises of these books, aimed, as they are, at younger readers.

Some examples of curriculum learning that was reasonably expected to come from these activities were:

(birth – 11 months) 'Have a positive approach to activities and experiences' – P,S&E
(40–60 months) 'enjoy listening to and using spoken language and readily turn to it in their play and learning' – C,L&L.
(8–24 months) 'Develop an awareness of number names through their enjoyment of action rhymes and songs that relate to their experience of numbers' – PS,R&N
(22–36 months) 'explore, play and seek meaning in their experiences' – KN&UW
(30–50 months) 'judge body space in relation to spaces available when fitting into confined spaces or negotiating openings and boundaries' – PD
(40–60 months) 'respond in a variety of ways to what they see, hear, smell and feel' – CD

It was felt that one of the major disadvantages to this topic was the lack of experience that children had of what a humid climate felt like and, thus, to imagine the lives of the people, plants and animals within this environment. It was at this point that a staff member remembered that the local botanic gardens had a tropical orchid house. A letter was written, a visit arranged and a group of the older children were taken to experience the tropics at first hand.

As it was January, the effect of the conditions inside the greenhouse on the children was powerful and immediate. Coats, gloves, hats and gloves were discarded and they were also instantly attracted to the colourful interior of the huge glasshouse. Here were flowering Bird of Paradise plants, Busy lizzies, better known to the children as summer bedding flowers, and a mass of vibrantly coloured orchids. Of huge interest were the carnivorous plants, the banana trees and the cocoa beans sitting in their cacao pods. Again, in the interest of accuracy, it should be pointed out that not all of what was seen on this visit necessarily grew in the type of rain forest that Mary was visiting, but it was felt that helping children to understand where, for example, chocolate came from, was too good an opportunity to miss. The guide showed the children the tropical pond with its water lilies and goldfish and then allowed them to select some huge leaves from the banana and palm trees to take back with them.

Back in the setting, some thinking was done as to where to begin the topic. Most children wanted to create a jungle, but there were varied ideas as to what they wanted it for. One group wanted a role-play area where they could dress up and creep through the jungle searching for crocodiles and insects, whereas others wanted a smaller interactive display which could have leaves at its base, vines climbing up the walls and their puppets and soft toys arranged in a 'small-world' play environment. The upshot was that one of each type of imaginative area was created, each with its own characteristics, and each used differently. The interactive display was formed on a table top which backed up against a window. On its base was strewn leaves, painted in a range of browns and yellows, and a blue silky scarf was laid through the leaves to create the river. Some exotic potted plants, ferns and evergreens, as well as a couple of carnivorous plants, were borrowed from parents and some vines were constructed in the workshop to climb to the tree canopy. The finishing touch was provided by a CD placed discreetly amongst the creepers which played the sounds of the jungle and created a realistic atmosphere. In the role-play area, the tree house that had been requested had, in the interests of safety, to be constructed at floor level and the imaginary crocodiles had, on occasions, to be reminded that they needed to stay in the designated lake area as they were sometimes in danger of becoming overenthusiastic in their hunt for human food! There were large palm trees constructed from cardboard, with leaves designed to match the ones brought back from the visit to the botanic garden, and spiders were made in the workshop and carefully placed amongst the trees. As in the case of other topics which needed role-play space, a home-play area was created well away from the excitements of the jungle for those children who needed the calm and the security of everyday home play.

As the desire for crocodiles was insatiable, it was decided that the children could design and make a crocodile from cardboard, with the teeth and scales being made from egg boxes. When painted and fixed to the wall there was great pride, but also some discussion, about him being rather lonely and a long way from his home in the jungle. Staff thought that the crocodile might provide a good writing opportunity and so it proved. When the children next arrived at the setting there was a letter from the crocodile announcing that he had come to live with them for a while. He was, he wrote, very gentle, but rather lonely and he had forgotten his name. Had the children any sugges-tions as to a name? He assured the children that he was a good writer and would reply to each letter he received.

For the full 8 weeks that the topic ran, children placed their letters, drawings and marks in the home-made postbox beside the crocodile and he was as good as his word, replying to each one. Staff needed to keep a weather eye on the postings to ensure that there was a name that could be deciphered on each piece of correspondence and did spend many off-duty hours replying to the children on the crocodile's behalf. However demanding it was on staff's time, it was the most enthusiastic that they had ever seen children (and in particular the boys) be about mark making and writing.

The produce of the rain forest provoked considerable interest, especially amongst those children who had visited the botanic gardens and seen the bananas and coconuts growing. Sensitive to the problems associated with nuts, these were not brought into the setting, but pictures of them were examined and some delicious tropical fruit salads constructed with the occasional grating of chocolate on the top. Some tropical seeds (such as avocado, lemon and orange) were grown, with mixed success, and exotic birds and insects looked up in books and painted. A large exotic frieze was designed and attached to one wall of the setting. Children contributed eagerly to this, painting palm trees, vines, snakes, spiders, butterflies, parrots and monkeys with great energy coupled with rather surprising accuracy. Some staff commented that they now understood why templates were counterproductive in a project such as this as they both hindered children's own creative ideas and did not always offer anything in the way of increased realism.

The younger children and those with particular learning needs who could not benefit from the full range of learning opportunities offered in the topic were carefully monitored by their key people to ensure that the learning provided in the setting was continuing to meet their developmental needs. It was with some surprise that staff reported that, according to their observations and assessments, the youngest children had enjoyed significant aspects of the topic, in particular the songs, rhymes and the musical instruments, mainly shakers, bells, drums and rain sticks, that had been intro-duced to accompany the jungle songs such as 'Oh, Mister Crocodile' and 'Swamp Wallowing'. They had tasted new fruits and heard new stories which had been offered alongside their everyday provision. Even the very youngest had watched the role play and enjoyed contributing to the larger areas of the frieze.

Discussions were had about the past and future of the rain forest and, in particular, the fact that it was so much at risk of destruction. The book *Window* provided a powerful, wordless illustration of the changes that can affect the rain-forest environment together with the creatures and people living there. *Oi, Get off Our Train*[207] was another book that tackled this subject matter and children showed a genuine concern and interest in the likely fate of endangered species.

There was great excitement when Mary's first photos came via the internet from the Daintree National Park. No, she had not yet spotted a crocodile but she had stood on the beach at the edge of the rain forest and seen wonderful shells and ancient vines climbing

'Dear snake, Where are you going? Jessica'

right up into the tall trees. Her journey was charted through the pages of *'Where the Forest Meets the Sea'*,[208] as this was the exact location of Mary's visit. She would bring us back some Australian animal songbooks and lots of photos illustrating her travels.

The project continued until Mary's return and then, quite naturally, came to an end. Many children were sad to see the crocodile go, but its purpose – forming a link to a much loved and absent key person – was at an end and much had been learned about other communities in the interim. The key lesson that the staff learned from this topic was to respect and abide by the principles of early childhood education, but be prepared to try out some different ideas. Trust your instincts, know your staff and children well and sometimes take a risk.

Endpiece

The major aim of this book has been to suggest ways in which practitioners can, through their relationships with their children, help them become effective learners. The theory chapters (in Section 1) contain some of the knowledge that practitioners need to teach in responsive ways and the practical chapters (in Section 2) have suggested how areas of the setting might look when the theories are implemented. The final chapter described some projects that combine the theory and practice, to give children rich, independent and cooperative learning experiences.

At the centre of this book has been the essential ingredient of relationships – hence the book's subtitle 'Responsive teaching and learning'. From the earliest days of traditional nursery education, adults have recognised the necessity of being responsive. The skills of active *listening*, of *observing* and of *following* children's interests are deeply rooted in sound educational theory. Being responsive rather than directive is an attitude of mind that needs to be acquired during training. It may be a hard skill to learn but it can be developed through watching children and then accepting that what is learned through observation will successfully inform teaching. By being responsive, practitioners are helping children in the best way they can by enabling independence, creativity, a sense of belonging and self-confidence. It is through these beginnings that democracies are built!

Robert Fulgham in his opening chapter of '*All I Need to Know I Learned in Kindergarten*'[209] suggested that the early years setting is a microcosm of life and that all that happens in an adult world is mirrored within the setting. It is up to us to ensure that our settings are responsive environments in which respect for ourselves, for each other and for the world in which we live has pride of place. We have great power to influence the children with whom we work; we need to use that power to demonstrate that the world can be a fair, exciting and loving place to inhabit.

References

1 Watt, Marion (2007) *Scaredy Squirrel*. Happy Cat Books!
2 Bruce,Tina (2005) *Early Childhood Education*, 3rd ed. Sevenoaks: Hodder Arnold.
3 Haddow (1931) *The Haddow Report*. London: HMSO.
4 Biddulph, Steve (2006) *Raising Babies*. Harper Thorsons.
5 Hanson, Kirstine and Hawkes, Denise (2009) Early childcare and child development. *Journal of Social Policy*. 38: 211–39.
6 DES (1990) *Starting with Quality (The Rumbold Report)*. London: Department of Education and Science, p 9, para 68.
7 National Association for the Education of Young Children. Position Statement 2009.
8 DfES (2007) *Early Years Foundation Stage*. London: DfES, Card 1.1.
9 Noddings, Nel (2003) *Happiness and Education*. Cambridge: Cambridge University Press.
10 All Our Futures, Creative and Cultural Education.
11 DfES (2004) *Every Child Matters. Changes for Children. Framework*. London: DfES.
12 See Ref 11, p 6.
13 See Ref 11, p 14.
14 Ball, Christopher *The Importance of Learning (Start Right Report)*. London: Royal Society for Arts, p 20.
15 *Childhood, Wellbeing and Primary Education*. Westminster Hall, March 2007.
16 Dowling, Marion (2000) *Young Children's Personal, Social and Emotional Development*. London: Paul Chapman Publishing.
17 DfES (2007) *Early Years Foundation Stage*. London: DfES.
18 Elfer, Peter, Goldschmied, Elinor and Sellick, Dorothy (2003) *Key Persons in the Nursery*. London: David Fulton, p 19.
19 Fonagy, Peter, Steele, M., Steele, H., Higgitt, Anna and Target, Mary (1995) *Journal of Child Psychology and Psychiatry*. 35(2): 231–57.
20 Davies, Bronwyn (1990) Agency as a form of discursive practice. A classroom scene observed. *British Journal of Sociology of Education*. 11: 341–61.
21 Roberts, Rosie (1995) *Self-Esteem and Early Learning*, London: Hodder and Stoughton, p 46.
22 Bruce, Tina (1991) *Time to Play in Early Childhood Education*. London: Hodder and Stoughton, p 108.
23 Katz, Lilian G. (1993) *Dispositions: Definitions and Implications for Early Childhood Practices*. Urbana, IL: ERIC Clearinghouse on Elementary and Early Childhood Education. Catalog #211; 47 pp.

24 Lindon, Jennie (2005) *Understanding Child Development, Linking Theory and Practice*. London: Hodder Arnold.

25 Fisher, Julie (1996) *Starting from the Child*. Buckingham: Open University Press, p 112.

26 www.answers.com.

27 Carr, Margaret (2001) *Assessment in Early Childhood Settings: Learning Stories*. London: Paul Chapman, p 88.

28 Bruner, Jerome (1976) The nature and uses of immaturity. In: Bruner, Jerome, Jolly, Alison and Sylva, Kathy (eds), *Play: Its Role in Development and Evolution*. New York: Basic Books.

29 DfES (2007) *Early Years Foundation Stage*. London: DfES, Card 4.3.

30 Donaldson, Margaret (1978) *Children's Minds*. London: Fontana.

31 Confucius. 551 BC to 479 BC.

32 DfES (2007) *Early Years Foundation Stage*. London: DfES.

33 Robinson, Maria (2010) *Understanding Behaviour and Development in Early Childhood*. Abingdon: Routledge.

34 DfES (2007) *Early Years Foundation Stage*. London: DfES, Card 4.3.

35 May, Pamela (2009) *Creative Development in the Early Year's Foundation Stage*. London: Routledge.

36 Shore, Rima (1997) *Rethinking the Brain*. New York: Families and Work Institute .

37 Watanabe, Shigeo (1993) *How do I Put It On*. London: Red Fox.

38 Garland, Sarah (1995) *Going to the Park*. London. Puffin books.

39 Meade, Anne and Cubey, Pam (1995) *Competent Children and Their Teachers*. Wellington: New Zealand Council for Educational Research.

40 Nutbrown, Cathy (2006) *Threads of Thinking*. London: Sage.

41 Unknown (1992) *Kindergarten Without Failure*. New Brunswick: Department of Education, Fredericton.

42 DfES (2007) *Early Years Foundation Stage*. London: DfES, Card 4.1.

43 EYFS pr 90.

44 Nurse, Angela (2009) *Physical Development in the Early Years Foundation Stage*. London: Routledge.

45 See Ref 24.

46 Robinson, Maria (2010) *Understanding Behaviour and Development in Early Childhood*. Abingdon: Routledge.

47 Goddard Blythe, Sally (2009) *Nursery World,* 3 December.

48 See Ref 47.

49 *Guardian* (2009) Thursday 30 December.

50 Goddard Blythe, Sally (2009) *Attention, Balance and Co-ordination – the A,B,C of Learning Success*. Wiley-Blackwell.

51 Bruner, Jerome (1983) *Child's Talk*. Oxford: Oxford University Press.

52 Nutbrown, Cathy (2006) *Threads of Thinking*. London: Sage.

53 Elfer, Peter, Goldschmeid, Elinor and Sellick, Dorothy (2003) *Key Persons in the Nursery: Building Relationships for Quality Provision*. London: David Fulton.

54 DfES (2007) *Early Years Foundation Stage*. London: DfES. Card: Learning and Development, Physical Development.

55 Darragh, Johanna C. (2006) The Environment as the Third Teacher. Eric Database No. ED 493517.

56 Karmiloff-Smith, Annette (1994) *Baby, It's You*. London: Ebury Press.

57 Gopnik, Alison, Melzoff, Andrew and Kuhl, Patricia (1999) *How Babies Think: The Science of Childhood*. London: Weidenfield and Nicolson.

58 *Guardian* (2010) Monday 4 January.

59 Murray, Lynn and Andrews, Liz (2000) *The Social Baby*. The Children's Project.

60 Roberts, Rosemary (1998) In: Iram Siraj-Blatchford (ed.) *A Curriculum Development Handbook for Early Childhood Decators*. Stoke on Trent: Trentham Books.

61 Vygotsky, Lev S. (1986) *Thought and Language*. Cambridge, MA: MIT.

62 Wells, Gordon (1987) *The Meaning Makers*. London: Hodder and Stoughton.

63 Pinker, Steven (1994) *The Language Instinct: The New science of Language and Mind*. Harmondsworth: Allen Lane/Penguin.

64 Bee, Helen (1997) *The Developing Child*. New York: Longman.

65 Tizzard, Barbara and Hughes, Martin (1984) *Young Children Learning: Talking and Thinking at Home*. London: Fontana.

66 Sylva, Kathy, Melhuish, Edward, Sammons, Pam, Siraj-Blatchford, Iram, Taggart, Brenda and Elliott, Karen (2003) *The Effective Provision of Preschool Education Project*. London: Institute of Education.

67 DfES (2007) *Early Years Foundation Stage*. London: DfES, Practice Guidance p 32.

68 See Ref 14.

69 DfES (2007) *Early Years Foundation Stage*. London: DfES, Practice Guidance p 34.

70 Robinson, Maria (2010) *Understanding Behaviour and Development in Early Childhood*. Abingdon: Routledge.

71 Lindon, Jennie (2005) *Understanding Child Development*. London: Hodder Arnold.

72 DfES (2007) *Early Years Foundation Stage*. London: DfES, Practice Guidance p 91.

73 DfES (2007) *Early Years Foundation Stage*. London: DfES, Practice Guidance p 90.

74 DfES (2007) *Early Years Foundation Stage*. London: DfES, Practice Guidance p 7.

75 Bruce, Tina (2006) *Early Childhood Education*. London: Hodder Arnold.

76 DfES (2007) *Early Years Foundation Stage*. London: DfES, Card 3.3.

77 Lindon, Jennie (2003) *Too Safe for Their Own Good? Helping Children Learn About Risks and Lifeskills*. London: National Children's Bureau.

78 DfES (2007) *Early Years Foundation Stage*. London: DfES, Practice Guidance p 23.

79 DfES (2007) *Early Years Foundation Stage*. London: DfES, Card 3.3.

80 Anon (1990) *Everything Has a Shadow Except Ants*. Commune De Reggio Emilia.

81 Robinson, Maria (2010) *Understanding Behaviour and Development in Early Childhood*. Abingdon: Routledge.

82 Waddell, Martin and Firth, Barbara (2001) *Can't You Sleep, Little Bear?* London: Walker Books.

83 See Ref 81.

84 Armitage, David and Armitage, Ronda (1994) *The Lighthouse Keeper's Lunch*. London: Scholastic.

85 DfES (2007) *Early Years Foundation Stage*. London: DfES Card 3.1.

86 DfES (2007) *Early Years Foundation Stage*. London: DfES, Practice Guidance p 78.

87 Goddard Blyth, Sally (2000) Mind and Body. *Nursery World*, 15 June 2000.

88 Bilton, Helen (2008) *Outdoor Play in the Early Years*. London: David Fulton.

89 See Ref 88.

90 See Ref 66.

91 Moser, Thomas and Foyn-Bruun, Emilie (2006) *The Pedagogical Foundations of Nature and Outdoor Kindergartens in Norway*. Reykjavik: EECERA.

92 See Ref 68.

93 Mackey, Glynne (2009) Ripples of Care Young children experience caring relationships in the outdoor environment. *Early Education*, Autumn, No. 59.

94 DfES (2007) *Early Years Foundation Stage*. London: DfES, Practice Guidance p 91.

95 DfES (2007) *Early Years Foundation Stage*. London: DfES, Practice Guidance p 53.

96 Brown, Ruth (1983) *A Dark, Dark Tale*. London: Scholastic.

97 Browne, Anthony (1989) *The Tunnel*. London: Walker Books.

98 Waddell, Martin (1991) *Once There Were Giants*. London: Walker Books.

99 Allen, Pamela (2003) *Grandpa and Thomas*. Harmondsworth: Penguin Books.

100 Alborough, Jez (2004) *Some Dogs Do*. London: Walker Books.

101 Jeffers, Oliver (2006) *Lost and Found*. London: Harper Collins.

102 Kent, Jack (1981) *There's No Such Thing as a Dragon*. Western Publishing Company.

103 Burningham, John (2004) *The Magic Bed*. London: Red Fox.

104 Munsch, Robert (1993) *The Paper Bag Princess*. London: Scholastic.

105 Trivizas, Eugene and Oxenbury, Helen (1993) *The Three Little Wolves and the Big Bad Pig*. Egmont.

106 Allen, Pamela (2001) *Brown Bread and Honey*. Harmondsworth: Penguin Books.

107 Sendak, Maurice (1980) *Where the Wild Things Are*. London: Puffin Books.

108 Murphy, Jill (1982) *On the Way Home*. London: Macmillan.

109 DfES (2007) *Early Years Foundation Stage*. London: DfES, Practice Guidance p 23.

110 See Ref 108.

111 Burningham, John (2001) *Mr Gumpy's Outing*. London: Red Fox.

112 Berenstain, Jan and Berenstain, Stan (1991) *Bears in the Night*. London: Harper Collins.

113 Donaldson, Julia (1999) *The Gruffalo*. London: Macmillan.

114 Hannon, Peter and Nutbrown, Cathy (1997) Raising early achievement in literacy teachers' use of a conceptual framework for early literacy education involving parents. *Teacher Development*. 1(3): 405–20.

115 Evangelou, Maria and Sylva, Kathy (2003) *The Effects of the Peers Early Education Partnership (PEEP) on Children's Developmental Progress*. London: Department for Education and Skills.

116 Meek, Margaret (1997) *On Being Literate*. London: The Bodley Head.

117 Briggs, Raymond (2003) *Jim and the Beanstalk*. London: Puffin Books.

118 Trivizas, Eugene (1997) *The Three Little Wolves and the Big, Bad Pig*. McElderry.

119 Cox, Brian (1989) *English for Ages Five to Sixteen*. London: Department of Education and Science, p 16.

120 Allen, Pamela (1980) *Mr Archimedes' Bath*. London: Penguin Books. Allen, Pamela (1992) *Alexander's Outing*. Victoria, Australia: Penguin Books.

121 See Ref 120.

122 Dowling, Paul (1998) *Beans on Toast*. London: Walker Books.

123 Carle, Eric (1985) *The Very Busy Spider*. Hamish Hamilton. Carle, Eric (1974) *The Very Hungry Caterpillar*. Picture Puffin.

124 Armitage, Ronda and Armitage, David (1994) *The Lighthouse Keeper's Lunch*. London: Scholastic.

125 Hardwick, Mairi (1985) *Katy Morag and the Wedding*. London: Red Fox.

126 Bruner, Jerome (1983) Child's talk: learning to use language. W.W. Norton., quoted in National Literacy Trust research (2009).

127 Kispal, Anne (2008) *Effective Teaching of Inference Skills for Reading: Literature Review*. DCSF Research Report 031. London: DCSF.

128 *Guardian* (2010) Tuesday 19 January.

129 Burningham, John (1978) *Time to Get Out of the Bath, Shirley*. London: Random House.

130 Hutchins, Pat (1968) *Rosie's Walk*. London: Red Fox.

131 See Ref 20.

132 See Ref 108.

133 DfES (1999) *All Our Futures*. London: National Advisory Committee on Creative and Cultural Education, p 4.

134 Hessell, Jenny (1990) *Staying at Sam's*. London: Harper Collins.

135 Moore, Inga (1996) *Six Dinner Sid*. London: Hodder.

136 Dodd, Lynley (2002) *Dogs Never Climb Trees*. London: Puffin Books.

137 Zion, Gene (1968) *Harry, The Dirty Dog*. Harmondsworth: Puffin Books.

138 See Ref 107.

139 Campbell, Rod (1982) *Dear Zoo*. London: Macmillan.

140 Burningham, John (1991) *Oi, Get off Our Train*. London: Red Fox.

141 Williams, Mo (2004) *Don't Let The Pigeon Drive the Bus*. London: Walker Books.

142 Sharratt, Nick (1994) *Ketchup on Your Cornflakes?* London: Scholastic.

143 Donaldson, Julia (2002) *Room on the Broom*. London: Macmillan.

144 Umansky, Kaye and Chamberlain, Margaret (1992) *Pass the Jam, Jim*. Bodley Head.

145 Sharrett, Nick (2007) *The Shark in the Park*. London: Random House.

146 Hutchins, Pat (1976) *Don't Forget The Bacon*. London: Random House.

147 DfES (2007) *Early Years Foundation Stage*. London: DfES, Practice Guidance p 104.

148 DfES (2007) *Early Years Foundation Stage*. London: DfES, Card 4.3.

149 Duffy, Bernadette (1988) *Supporting Creativity and Imagination in the Early Years*. Buckingham: Open University Press, p 77.

150 DfES (2007) *Early Years Foundation Stage*. London: DfES, Practice Guidance p 110.

151 DfES (2007) *Early Years Foundation Stage*. London: DfES, Practice Guidance p 104.

152 Laevers, Ferre (1996) The Leuven Involvement Scale for Young Children, Centre for Experiential Education, Leuven, Belgium.

153 May, Pamela (2000) Water play in early years settings. Unpublished MA. Oxford: Brookes University.

154 Carle, Eric (1995) *The Very Hungry Caterpillar*. London: Puffin Books.

155 Roberts, R. (2006) *Companionable Research at Home with Birth to Threes*. European Early Childhood Education Association Conference Iceland.

156 DfES (2007) *Early Years Foundation Stage*. London: DfES, Card 1.2.

157 Malaguzzi, Loris (1993) The hundred languages of children. In: C. Edwards, L. Gandini and G. Forman (eds), *The Hundred Languages of Children. The Reggio Emilia Approach – Advanced Reflections*. Greenwich, CT: Ablex.

158 See Ref 157.

159 See Ref 44.

160 DfES (2007) *Early Years Foundation Stage*. London: DfES, Practice Guidance p 107.

161 See Ref 140.

162 Carr, Margaret (2007) *Assessment in Early Childhood Settings*. London: Sage, p 98.

163 See Ref 68.

164 Duffy, Bernadette (1998) *Supporting Creativity and Imagination in the Early Years*. Buckingham: Open University Press.

165 Dunn, Judith (1995) *Cognition and Emotion, Connections Between Understanding and Development*. Hove: Laurence Earlbaum Associates.

166 Grahame, Kenneth (2007) *The Wind in the Willows*. London: Penguin Classics.

167 Allen, Pamela (1990) *Who Sank the Boat?* London: Puffin Books.

168 See Ref 111.

169 Gussin Paley, Vivian (2001) *In Mrs Tulley's Room: A Childcare Portrait*. Cambridge, MA: Harvard University Press.

170 Manning-Morton, Julia and Thorp, Maggie (2001) *Key Times*. *A Framework for Providing High Quality Provision for Children Under Three Years Old*. London: Print Emporium Ltd. Camden Early Years Under Threes Development Project.

171 Bruce, Tina (1991) *Time to Play in Early Childhood Education*. London: Hodder and Stoughton.

172 Meek, Margaret (1985) Play and paradoxes: some considerations of imagination and language. In: C.G Wells and J. Nicholls, (eds), *Language and Learning, an Interactional Perspective*. Buckingham: Open University Press.

173 Chambers, Aiden (1993) *Tell Me: Reading and Talk*. Stroud: Thimble Press.

174 DfES (2007) *Early Years Foundation Stage*. London: DfES, Card 4.3.

175 See Ref 66.

176 DfES (2007) *Early Years Foundation Stage*. London: DfES, Practice Guidance p 32.

177 DfES (2007) *Early Years Foundation Stage*. London: DfES, Card 4.3.

178 Said by a 5 year old in a setting.

179 DfES (2007) *Early Years Foundation Stage*. London: DfES, Card 4.3.

180 DfES (2007) *Early Years Foundation Stage*. London: DfES, Practice Guidance p 58.

181 DfES (2007) *Early Years Foundation Stage*. London: DfES, Card 1.1.

182 Anon. Widely quoted on the internet.

183 See Ref 24.

184 Whitehed, M. (1999). *Supporting Language and Literacy Development in the Early Years*. Buckingham: Open University Press.

185 DfES (2007) *Early Years Foundation Stage*. London: DfES, Practice Guidance p 102.

186 DfES (2007) *Early Years Foundation Stage*. London: DfES, Practice Guidance p 79.

187 DfES (2007) *Early Years Foundation Stage*. London: DfES, Card 3.3.

188 Cousins, Jacqui (1999) *Listening to Four Year Olds*. The National Early Years Network.

189 DfES (2007) *Early Years Foundation Stage*. London: DfES, Card 4.3.

190 Gura, Pat (1992) *Exploring Learning: Young Children and Blockplay*. London: Paul Chapman Educational Publishing.

191 DfES (2007) *Early Years Foundation Stage*. London: DfES, Card 4.3.

192 See Ref 50.

193 Moyles, Janet (1990) *The Excellence of Play*. Buckingham: Open University Press.

194 Awdry, Reverend Wilbert (1946) *Thomas the Tank Engine*. London: Edmund Ward.

195 DfES (2007) *Early Years Foundation Stage*. London: DfES, Practice Guidance p 74.

196 DfES (2007) *Early Years Foundation Stage*. London: DfES, Card 3.3.

197 Moss, Peter in Paige-Smith, A. and Craft, A. (eds) (2008) *Developing Reflective Practice in the Early Years. Buckingham*: Open University Press.

198 Fortunati, Aldo (2006) *The Education of Young Children as a Community Project*. Azzano san Paulo: Edizoni Junior.

199 DfES (2007) *Early Years Foundation Stage*. London: DfES, Practice Guidance p 40.

200 DfES. (2007) *Early Years Foundation Stage*. London: DfES, Practice Guidance p 86.

201 Waddel, Martin (1991) *And Then There Were Giants*. London: Walker Books.

202 Anning, Angela and Edwards, Anne (1999) *Promoting Children's Learning from Birth to Five*. Buckingham: Open University Press.

203 Baker, Jeannie (2002) *Window* and (1989) *Where the Forest Meets the Sea*. London: Walker Books.

204 Rose, Gerald (2001) *Ahhhh! Said the Stork*. Cambell Books.

205 West, Colin (1998) *Have You Seen the Crocodile*. London: Walker Books.

206 Lacombe, Julie (1995) *Walking Through the Jungle*. London: Walker Books.

207 See Ref 140.

208 See Ref 203.

209 Fulgham, Robert (1990) *All I Need to Know I Learned in Kindergarten*. New York. Ballantine Books.

Author Index

Subject Index